Appreciative Inquiry

As a

Potent Strategy

for

Empowering Christian Women

Dr. Passy Anayo Amaraegbu

e-mail-drpassy@yahoo.com

ISBN
978-978-959-099-5

Published by
Wisdom Literary & Management Agency,
wisdomliterary@gmail.com
+2348034745556

Graphic Concept + Design: David O. Okoduwa

Except otherwise stated all scriptural quotations are from the New King James Version (NKJV) of the Holy Bible.

Dedicated To:

Resourceful Justina Onuigbo my mother
Resilient Chimezie Cecilia my wife
Radiant Jerushah Amarachi our first daughter
Resolute Queen Esther Chidiebere our last child.

CONTENTS

Tables

Tables

ACKNOWLEDGEMENTS

My first gratitude goes to God for His mercy and faithfulness in helping me enroll and complete the Doctor of Ministry Program at Bakke Graduate University. Truly, His thoughts are deeper than the ocean, and His ways are mysterious. To Him be all the glory and honor.

Thank you to my wonderful wife, pharmacist Chimezie, and godly children, Nwachukwu, Jedidiah, Jerushah, Jachukwumma, and Queen Esther, I say a big thank you for all the sacrifice of time and other resources that provided a conducive atmosphere for me to work. The same appreciation goes to office staff at Charismatic Renewal Ministries, Lagos State, Nigeria. These are, Pastor Ignatius Ihejirika, Julius Osazee, Felix Chima, Paulinus Ngumah, and Julius Nwachukwu. Kemi Matthew deserves an exceptional appreciation for her indefatigable computer assistance.

Thank you to the Bakke Graduate University team of Carolyn Cochran, Judi Melton, Lowell Bakke, and Brad Smith, I am most grateful for diverse input and assistance. Martine Audeoud, my supervisor, Bill Payne, my research method lecturer; and Randy White, my Overtures I and II lecturer. I appreciate their special roles in my completing the program.

Finally, I thank my mentors and parents in the Lord, Cosmas and Adeola Ilechukwu, for their various assistance and exemplary leadership style. Also my appreciation goes to Dave Inyere, who on various occasions helped me to secure some literature. Emma and Nkem Nwachukwu, Christy Olowogbemi, Francis Ogunsusi, Tunde Makinde, Sunny Orere, and Marcel Udebuani, are some of my associate pastors whose help at various stages of the research work were significant. Thank you all and God bless.

ABSTRACT

The purpose of this study was to empower Christian women through the strategy of Appreciative Inquiry. The population was women of Charismatic Renewal Ministries and the male leadership in Lagos State, Nigeria, while the sample consisted of those in two of the branches of the church in Lagos State. The scope of the study included discovering the source as well as forms of marginalization of women in order to establish the specific areas of women's life to employ the Appreciative Inquiry Strategy.

An overview of the beliefs, groupthink, and perceptions of both genders in the church revealed the common challenges women face in typical African churches. These challenges women face in African churches include disparity in honor, exercise of ecclesiastical authority, and remuneration between male and female ministers as well as opportunities to occupy top leadership positions. While some churches are improving on these sensitive issues as relating to women, others are yet to commence any form of progress.

The study established the theological principle that women have equal opportunity to manifest their God-given gifts and abilities. Whenever women were (are) given opportunity as well as encouraged to perform in accordance to their gifts and skills, they did (do) so excellently. In creating a woman, God never intended to clone another male gender. The Creator was intentional, purposeful, and decisive. Consequently there is a great need to encourage and challenge women to be their best. Among the male dominated church and society leadership, a positive step towards women empowerment would mean to jettison the traditional African mindset of marginalizing women and become renewed in their minds.

The descriptive qualitative research tools of interviews and questionnaires were used for the study, and the research findings were consistent with study objectives. Accordingly, the methodology confirmed that the Charismatic Renewal Ministries Lagos State leadership were actively engaged in women empowerment programs. Also the result revealed a significant difference in the worldview of both male and females in the church.

The result of the study revealed a renewed call to adopt a paradigm shift for both genders. The men would need to appreciate the uniqueness and value of women more, while the women would need to release themselves from psychological chain of inferiority complex occasioned by an age long practice of marginalization. I recommended that to achieve this great milestone of optimum empowerment of women, the educational and enlightenment programs for both genders should begin early in childhood as well remain consistent. Finally greater opportunities should be provided for women to gain quality education as well as evolve a career policy that offers equitable opportunity to women to rise to an upper echelon of their careers in the church and society.

CHAPTER 1

INTRODUCTION

Appreciative Inquiry as a potent strategy for empowering Charismatic Women is founded on proven research findings.[1] It is akin to the principle of reciprocity whereby there exists a positive correlation or congruency between the seed and the harvest. In other words, love breeds more love, while hatred produces more wickedness. In the same manner, marginalization of women breeds more marginalization, while appreciation is likely to lead to more appreciation. In an earlier study on Christian women, I made the case that the leadership of the church would benefit immensely from the women folk if the former exchanges the strategy of marginalization with appreciation by including women in church leadership positions.[2]

Mensah and Mensah comment that life thrives and blossoms in an atmosphere of love and care.[3] Therefore, I believe that, appreciation, acceptance, affirmation and affection constitute the conductive atmosphere which oils the wheel of our earthly existence. Conversely, life shrivels and shrinks and mortals sink into the mud when they are continuously exposed to despise, denigration and degradation. Unfortunately, the female folk have suffered all forms of degradation and denigration in several societies and sects, countries and communities. A useful input, may suffice here

Generally speaking, the image of women is rather low among the Nigerian ethnic groups surveyed. The majority of the respondents indicated that the concept of woman is quite inferior. She is looked

---

[1] Sue Annis Hammond, *The Thin Book of Appreciative Inquiry* (Plano, TX: Thin Book Pub Co, 1998).

[2] Passy Amaraegbu, "Appreciative Inquiry of Charismatic Renewal Ministries Women,"[final paper in *Overture 2: Fresno* class, Fresno, CA: Bakke Graduate University, October 2013].

[3] Joseph Mensah and Francisca Mensah, *Kingdom Principles for Success in Marriage* (Ibadan, Nigeria: Inspiration House Publishing, 2011).

upon as the source of sexual satisfaction for man. One of the respondents wrote, "women are just like man's property... being treated just like slaves... like what the husband bought with money.[4]

Such maltreatment of the female folk is barbaric and horrific. One wonders whether such ugly experiences are repeated in the churches in Nigeria. Particularly, is there evidence of marginalization of women in the Charismatic Renewal Ministries, Lagos State? If so, what are the particular areas of female marginalization?

On the other hand, are there proofs of women empowerment and appreciation in the Charismatic Renewal Ministries, Lagos State? How can I help to encourage greater improvement of women empowerment in the church?

This chapter provides the context of the problem being investigated. Beginning with understanding the traditional African or Nigerian mindset of limited freedom for the female folk, (which partly accounts for the marginalization of women), it proceeds to define the problem statement, outlines the objectives of the study, as well as provides reasons for carrying out the study. The other important aspects of the study include statement of my hypothesis, specification of the audience as well as the research limitations and delimitations.

The research was carried out among the top leadership echelon and women in two branches of Charismatic Renewal Ministries, Lagos State, Nigeria: Dominion Center, Egbe and Holy Ghost Church, Surulere, both in Lagos State, Nigeria.

Background of the Problem

Gender-related issues are usually passionate and potent. They affect both minor and major, convert and overt spheres of human existence. Consequently, sexuality is one of the most fundamental passions in the life of humanity.[5]

---

[4] Danfulani Zamani Kore, *Culture and the Christian Home: Evaluating Cultural Marriage and Family in Light of Scriptures* (Jos, Nigeria: ACTS University of Jos, 3, 1995). Quoted in Lawrence Ettu, A Female Adults in the church (Owerri, Nigeria: Charismatic Forum Publications Limited, 2000), 36.

[5] Passy Amaraegbu, *Victory over Lust: Key to Victorious Living* (Lagos, Nigeria: Change Business Services, Ltd., 1995).

Nigeria with an estimated population of 178.6 million people[6] is constituted of 48.79 percent of females and 51.21 percent of males.[7] This population ratio of male and female Nigerians, though equitable, may be the only index or measure of near equitability of the genders because inequality parades other spheres of gender-related issues. For instance, between 1988-1991 in a population of 4,243 top managers in the Nigerian Federal Civil Service the percentage of male Nigerians was 88.6 percent while the female was 11.35 percent [8] Obviously the skewed inequality against the female folk is significantly overwhelming. Olojede's study confirms the issue of marginalization of women in the Nigerian society.[9]

In the context of the church, the Charismatic Renewal Ministries, Lagos State, Nigeria, the two issues of women marginalization and empowerment are interrelated. In some areas, the females are recognized, honored, and empowered. Examples of the areas where my church shows positive value towards women include encouraging them to acquire education, develop their gifts and pursue their careers. Yet in some other areas like giving female ministers equal honor and remuneration as their fellow male counterparts, my church need to improve.

Appreciative Inquiry was the method of choice in this study. It was used to identify the areas where this church already empowers the females as well as those where the church leadership and membership needed to engage in more empowerment schemes for the women.

Statement of the Problem

This dissertation focused on the marginalization of Charismatic Renewal Ministries women in Lagos State, Nigeria. It sought to

---

[6] World Population Review, "Nigeria Population 2014," http://worldpopulationreview.com/countries/nigeria-population/ (accessed September 6, 2014).

[7] Veracity, "Nigerian Census - Gender Population Distributon Shift, a Red Flag," http://nigerianpolity.blogspot.com/2007/01/nigerian-census-gender-population.html (accessed September 7, 2014).

[8] Olojede, "Women: The Neglected Force in Public Administration," quoted in Jacob Olufemi Fatile, Adejuwon David, and Kehinde David, "Gender Issues in Human Resource Management in Nigerian Public Service," *African Journal of Political Science and International Relations* Vol. 5, no. 3 (March 2011): 112-119.

[9] Ibid. p.114

discover specific examples of this marginalization such as discrimination in leadership position, low ministerial remuneration, limited opportunity to serve, and a general lower regard for the feminine gender. Furthermore, I studied this crucial issue in order to catalyze transformation among Charismatic Women who would experience a significant change from marginalization to empowerment. The study also considered the significant negative impact of culture, illiteracy, and religious practices as well as government policy on the subject matter of women marginalization.

Research Objectives

The main objective of this research is to catalyze transformation in the lives of Charismatic Women through Appreciation Inquiry. The objectives of the research follow:

1.   to establish the various issues of marginalization among Charismatic Women in Lagos State, Nigeria

2.   to discover the degree of Women empowerment in the Charismatic Renewal Ministries, Lagos State

3.   to discover what can be done to encourage the church leadership to further develop empowerment programs for the Charismatic Women

4.   to suggest both to the Charismatic leadership and membership ways to improve in empowering the Charismatic Women in Lagos State, Nigeria.

Definitions of Key Words and Terms

Appreciative Inquiry is an alternative research approach which focuses on the existing strengths and positive proofs of the investigated variables or factors in the research context for the purpose of utilizing them to catalyze transformation. The basic assumption of Appreciative Inquiry is that in every organization,"something works and that change can be managed through the identification of what works and the analysis of how to do more of what works"[10]

Empowerment is a process of raising the powerless to a position of joint co- creative power. Empowerment is a restoration process to provide enablement to the disadvantaged or marginalized. It is

---

[10] Hammond, 3.

bringing the marginalized to a state of shalom. The connection between empowerment and shalom (a state of well-being) is a positive correlation. In other words, empowered people will be more likely to enjoy a state of well-being. The Hebrew word *shalom* is difficult to define, but the word could mean amongst other things "total well-being" or "restoration."[11]

Charismatic Renewal Ministries Incorporated is a Pentecostal church which is an offshoot from the Nigerian Catholic Charismatic Movement. It began as a students' campus fellowship in 1980 at the erstwhile University of Ife, Ile – Ife, Oyo State, Nigeria (now Obafemi Awolowo University) but became an independent church in 1999. It has over 550 branches in 34 out of the 36 states and federal capital of Nigeria and some African countries. The Charismatic Renewal Ministries also has branches in the United States, Europe, and Asia. The term *Charismatic Women* refers to both the matured single ladies and married females in the twenty-two branches of the Lagos church.

Research Question

The main research question for this dissertation is as follows: What are the challenges the leadership of Charismatic Renewal Ministries, Lagos State, Nigeria, face while empowering women in their churches, and how can the leadership be significantly assisted in developing further empowerment opportunities for women?

Research Sub-Questions

The study will also address the following questions.

1. In what ways are women marginalized in Charismatic Renewal Ministries, Lagos State?

2. How does predominant culture contribute to the issue of marginalization?

3. What are the proofs or evidence of women empowerment in Charismatic Renewal Ministries, Lagos State?

4. What practical strategies are available to address the challenges of women empowerment?

---

[11] Lowell Bakke, "A Letter to Rowanna" (lecture, Overture: Fresno, Bakke Graduate University, Fresno, CA, October 2013).

Hypotheses

The major presupposition of this research is that Appreciative Inquiry is the method of choice for achieving women empowerment among Charismatic Women. Based on this assumption, the following hypotheses are made.

1.   Males and Females who participated in the Appreciative Inquiry intervention process will differ in their views on the issue of women empowerment.

2.   Male leaders will obtain significantly lower scores than their female counterparts in all the measures of women empowerment.

Research Design, Research Instruments and Data Analysis

This research presupposed that Appreciative Inquiry was the appropriate approach for empowering Charismatic Women. Therefore data was collected using the questionnaire and interview format of AI, while data was analyzed using the social science statistical package and two-way Analysis of variance (ANOVA). The two variables of interests here were gender and the level of empowerment. Since ANOVA tests the differences between two or more means, the means of these two variables (gender and empowerment) were the focus of statistical analysis.

Audience

Starting with my Personal Learning Community, the leaders of the local assembly of Charismatic Renewal Ministries, Surulere, Lagos, will be the primary readers of this dissertation.   Others include the following.

1.   members and leaders of Charismatic Renewal Ministries in Lagos State and national headquarters

2.   people in the economic sector such as bankers and microfinance workers

3.   people in the private, public, and government services

4.   community and opinion leaders

5.   Bake Graduate University community

Stakeholders

The people and organizations that will have vested interest in this project include the following.

1.   the State and Regional Core Group of the Charismatic Renewal Ministries in Lagos and South West Nigeria

2. the General Core Group of Charismatic Renewal Ministries Worldwide
3. financial institutions
4. non-government institutions in Lagos like Centre for Marriage and Family Stability and Missions Aid International
5. the various church women's groups
6. my wife, pharmacist Chimezie Passy-Amaraegbu, who understands the vision of women empowerment

Scope and Limitations

One of the limitations of this study was the sample. It focused on the women-folk of Charismatic Renewal Ministries Lagos State from which population the sample was drawn. Yet, this population is just one out of the thirty-four states plus the capital territory in Nigeria where the Charismatic Renewal Ministries exists. There were possible other limitations such as lack of cooperation with the sample audience. At, the appropriate time they were needed to respond to the questionnaires and interview sessions, economic cost of carrying out the project, and the possibility of resistance against conducting the study from some male leaders who may feel threatened by the result of the study. Possibly too, my masculine status might also stand as a limitation to the study.

Delimitations

The study guarded against bias by employing the services of graduate level and well-trained assistants in the distribution of the questionnaires and interviews. Also the Analysis of Variance (ANOVA) statistic was used to enhance the result of the study.

The Outcome of the Study

Beginning with the females in the church, this study discovered the diverse forms of women marginalization as well as empowerment among Charismatic Renewal Ministries Churches in Lagos State, Nigeria. It revealed the level of the reality of the issues being speculated or presumed.

Integration with Various Dimensions of Transformational Leadership

The project addressed transformational leadership perspectives in the following concrete ways.

1. Calling-Based Leadership. One has a strong conviction in carrying out such a project in a significantly disadvantaged environment against women. This project served like a call to fulfill destiny.

2. Incarnational Leadership. I cannot transform into a woman but can and do identify with the pains of the female-folk in the church and society. The oppression of one equals that of the whole body. Hopefully too, the liberation of one equals that of others.

3. Reflective Leadership. Through meditative thought this project postulated that oppression and all forms of injustice would never last forever. Therefore, it was better to be part of the solution than to continue to stand on the fence or remain part of the problem.

4. Servant Leadership. Very significantly, exemplary living is the best way to catalyze change. This project therefore strongly promotes the ideal servant leadership style by boldly reaching out to uplift the downtrodden women-folk through service and care for their needs.

5. Contextual Leadership. The beginning of the empowerment program among these Christian women was to understand the peculiar ways both marginalization and empowerment existed in their context. The research was built on the issues of women marginalization and empowerment.

6. Global Leadership. In today's world, variously referred to as "global village" and "city," the central issues in this project were women marginalization and empowerment in the church .Therefore, the project sought to reflect both local and global trends.

7. Shalom Leadership. Reconciliation of relationships is at the core of this project. This involved reconciliation of the church leadership with God for marginalizing their women-folk, between the male and female-folks and also between the female and God for being resentful of God and possibly of the male.

8. Prophetic Leadership. This project involved speaking to power. Normally this involved speaking to the male dominated team of both local assembly and other cadres of Christian leaders. The virtues of humility and love were wisely applied.

Summary

Chapter one of the study constituted pieces of information about the background, problem statement, research objectives and questions, hypotheses, outcome, audience, contributions to transformational leadership, limitations, and delimitations. Chapter two will focus on the context, historical background, and the current situation of women empowerment in the Charismatic Renewal Ministries, Lagos State, Nigeria.

CHAPTER 2

CONTEXT OF THE PROJECT

Historical Background

The Charismatic Renewal Ministries Incorporated began on February 18, 1980, as a Catholic charismatic students fellowship on campus. The Renewal Ministry began with seven undergraduate students from the former University of Ife (now Obafemi Awolowo University) Ile-Ife, Oyo State, Nigeria. Their names are Adeola Ilechukwu, Bukola Atolagbe (both nee Olugunna), Bridget Azigbo, Obiora Nwosu, Magnus Mbajoirgu, Peter Ezekwenna, and Cosmas Ilechukwu. Very remarkably, each of them had a personal conviction to gather together to pray sacrificially and in an organized manner for the salvation of fellow Catholics in the 1979/80 academic year. When they finally gathered together to pray, they amazingly confirmed that their individual personal convictions to come together to pray was divinely prompted.[1]

The Lagos branch of the ministry began in 1984 with a few graduates who came to Lagos for the purpose of engaging in the compulsory one-year National Youths Service program and a few others at the University of Lagos, Akoka. From one branch in 1984, the ministry has grown to twenty-two branches in 2014. Also the ministry has grown from eight youths in 1984 to a membership of over three thousand adults in 2014. Of this adult membership, the women constitute about half of the population.[2]

---

[1] Austen C. Ukachi, *The Best Is yet to Come: Pentecostal and Charismatic Revivals in Nigeria From 1914 to 1990s* (Nigeria: Summit Press, Ltd., 2013).

[2] Passy Amaraegbu, "A Short History of the Ministry in Lagos State" (lecture, 25th Anniversary of the Ministry, Lagos State, Nigeria, November, 15, 2009).

In the present circumstance, there is evidence of marginalization of the women-folk in the Charismatic Renewal Ministries such as limited scope for ordained women ministers and lesser remuneration in service. From the early days of the ministry on campus, the issue of marginalization of the female-folk was in existence but might not have been obvious. Truly the Charismatic Renewal Ministries had always had women ministers in the church, but the ratio of the male to female representation in the highest leadership echelon has always been negatively skewed against the latter. Remarkably, in three decades, the National body of Charismatic Renewal Ministries had only one female State Overseer (formerly, Representative), and that was in the early years of the ministry. It seems that as the ministry becomes institutionalized and established, the level of marginalization against the female-folk increased. Presently, there is no female State Overseer. In times past, Lagos State had a female Center (Parish) pastor, but not at present. Instead, some of the senior female pastors are involved in supervisory roles at the zonal level.

One plausible reason for the increase in the marginalization of the female-folk in the ministry currently can be attributed to the development of family life cycle. Before getting married, the female-folk had more time and energy to concentrate on the work of the ministry, but as the responsibilities of marriage and homemaking arrived, the female-folk, being the primary agents of making a home, necessarily began to give more attention to marriage and family matters. The other side of the story is that from my observation, both African Culture and the male-folk prefer this arrangement whereby the management of the home front is predominantly consigned to the women folk.

Perhaps in the latter stage of the family cycle when the children are grown up (empty nest stage), Charismatic women will regain their prominent positions in ministry. However, this assumption is only my speculation, and there is a great need to highlight as well as find a godly solution to this problem of marginalization of women in the church. In the light of these challenges, this project utilized Appreciative Inquiry to transform these ugly situations. The basic

11

premise of Appreciative Inquiry is that, everybody has the capacity, expertise, and resources that an alternative inquiry requires.[3]

Background of Nigerian Society

Women marginalization is a common feature in Africa, nay, Nigeria. In almost every sphere of home life, business, government, and even religious places, the Nigerian female is considered as being inferior to her male counterpart.[4] This ugly attitude transcends the various tribes and tongues, cultures, and communities in Nigeria. For instance, traditionally among the three major tribes of Hausa, Igbo, and Yoruba, polygamy is permitted and even encouraged, yet polyandry is regarded as an abomination.[5] Some of the reasons for the prevalence of polygamy in Nigeria include the search for male children who will both fight wars as well as continue the family lineage, provision of labour force for the farm lands, and raising economic insurance for the future.

Unfortunately all these reasons for polygamy in Nigeria place the female folk in a disadvantageous position. They were (still are) marginalized. A researcher captures the Nigerian situation of female marginalization when he noted,

It is a well-known fact that the culture of a people has a great impact on their attitude and behavioural patterns. Therefore, the root cause of the psychological problems of women may be traced back to the cultural stands of most people with regard to women. The erroneous idea that women are not as important as men, or rather that women are inferior to men.[6]

---

[3] Peter Block, *Community: The Structure of Belonging* (San Francisco: Berrett-Koehler Publishers, 2008).

[4] Emmanuel Obasi, "Discrimination against Women and Marginalization in Nigerian Politics," Gistarea, http://www.gistarea.com/discrimination-women-marginalization-nigeria-politics (accessed August 15, 2014).

[5] Stanislaw Krolewiec, "Black People: A History of World Polyandry" http://detestee. Com/threads/a history-of-world-polyandry. 371131 (Accessed May 9, 2016).

[6] Lawrence O. Ettu, *A Christian Response to the Problems of Single Female Adults in the Church* (Owerri, Nigeria: Charismatic Renewal Ministries, Inc., 2000). 20.

Who are the custodians of the society's culture? Who are the kings and kingmakers in Africa? Most often, they are predominantly men. Consequently since these African men are significantly involved in the marginalization of women, I believe that it is only fair for us to be involved in the empowerment and restoration process of females too.

Another major form of women marginalization in Nigeria is human trafficking.

The trafficking of children for the purpose of domestic service is a widespread phenomenon in Nigeria. Children and women are recruited with promises of well-paid jobs in urban centres within the country or abroad, realizing too late that they have been lured into a debt bond. Violence, coercion and deception are used to take victims away from their families. Regretfully Nigeria is a source, transit and destination country for trafficked women and children.[7]

I believe the trafficking of children is an obnoxious and wicked practice, yet these twin evils of merchandizing children and women go on unabated[8]. This is one of the reasons I am engaging in this dissertation so as to raise a voice against this evil and seek for the appropriate remedy.

Current Situation

In Africa, marginalization of women is commonplace, both in the church and society.[9]Also in the developed worlds of Europe and America, the issue of women marginalization does exist in different dimensions, which has necessitated the emergence of diverse forms of women liberation programs.[10] Examples of women marginalization in Nigeria include the following:

---

[7] UNICEF, "Child Trafficking," http://www.unicef.org/nigeria/children_1939.html (accessed April 1, 2014).

[8] UNICEF, Ibid.

[9] Patience Ita Hove, "The Copious Challenges Faced by Women in Leadership in the Zimbabwean Society" (DTL dissertaton, Bakke Graduate University, 2012).

[10] William H. Wilde, Joy W. Hooton, and Barry Andrews, *The Oxford Companion to Australian Literature* (Melbourne: Oxford University Press, 1994), 271.

1. restricted opportunities in the marketplace and career choices
2. poor representation in both political and spiritual leadership
3. the abandonment of parenting responsibilities to mothers during the early stage of the child
4. the promotion of negative attitudes towards women such as despising, disregard, and devaluation of their contributions at home, church and society
5. male insensitive behavior towards the health of women (mothers) who are in the critical stage of child bearing (This is manifest in such poor male attitudes like poor spacing of children as well frequency of pregnancy which endangers both the health of the mother and child)

It is therefore the goal of this project to discover and proffer pragmatic solutions to these crucial challenges.

Relevant Personal, Organizational and Global Issues:

The two issues that this thesis addresses, namely, women marginalization and empowerment have both local and international dimensions. Neither males nor females are immune to misunderstanding of each other, but the female gender may be bearing the greater consequences of this anomaly. Cole makes the following assertion: "Women desire their men to make decisions. Not as a dictator, but as a leader. There is a vast difference. Dictators make decisions based on personal preferences or selfish gratification, but leaders make decisions based on what is best for their followers."[11] Cole's statement takes it for granted that men should always lead women. The statement also does take into consideration that the leadership skill of men are limited in certain areas. In other words depending on the sphere of life, both men and women can exhibit leadership skills. What qualifies such a statement as being significantly marginalizing against women is the normative and assumptive stand of such a twenty-first century minister of the Gospel like Cole.[12]

---

[11] Edwin Louis Cole, *Maximized Manhood* (Port Harcourt, Nigeria: Outreach Christian Bookcentres, 2003), 71.

[12] Ibid.

14

From a personal vantage point, I cherish the immense advantages I am enjoying because of my relationship with empowered women such as my high school teacher mother, pharmacist wife, and several others who helped and still help me to strive to achieve my utmost in life. My mother after the birth of five children went back to school to train as a teacher. My wife, though the youngest among three of her sisters, is the first female graduate and the second in a home of seven siblings. These testimonials are both relevant and important to me because they act as springboards for me to strive to empower my two daughters and every other woman I encounter. Also, my parents' compulsory policy of provision of equal opportunity for the education of both male and female children has motivated several other families in my community to strive to educate their girl children in particular.

In contrast to this trend, one notable and agonizing aspect of women marginalization in most African societies is that of denial of rights of widows. Marriages contracted under the customary court legacy expose widows to horrible hardship and neglect to the point that they are denied access to their husbands' property. The surviving male members of the extended family determine both the state of the widow and ownership of the deceased property. "Under customary marriage, the widows form part of the estate of their husbands."[13] I believe this cultural norm is an extreme form of marginalization of the female-folk.

The issue of human trafficking has grown deeper, from being a local to an international problem. Nigeria is implicated as a source, transit, and destination point for both children and women. Children and women are lured away or in some cases abducted from Nigeria and trafficked to other African countries such as Gabon, Cameroon, Ghana, Chad, Benin, Togo, Niger, Burkina Faso, Gambia, and outside Africa to countries like Italy, Russia, and Middle East for the purposes of forced labour and prostitution.[14]

---

[13] Ify Amasiatu, *Legal Challenges to Christian Life* (Port Harcourt: Nebo Christian Services, , 2012, 34.

[14] UNICEF, "Child Trafficking" Ibid.

15

At other times, children and women are brought into Nigeria from other African countries particularly those in the west African region for the same purpose. These wicked acts easily go on undetected due to easy access to the borders of these West African countries.

Worse still, is the Boko Haram Islamic sect policy of waging an unholy war against the acceptance of Western education. This Islamic sect's hatred for education and women empowerment attained a notorious degree when they kidnapped over two hundred high school girls in Bornu State, Nigeria.[15] Today (August 5, 2014) is the 113th day since these young girls who were assured of safety by their state government to return to school and participate in the West African and Examination Council Exam were lured and abducted by the members of the Islamic insurgents. Two years after (May 9, 2016), the update in this sordid story of abduction is that out of the two hundred and seventy six girls, fifty seven of them escaped the same day and the remaining two hundred and nineteen are yet to be recovered. The attitude of the new federal government in Nigeria towards the recovery of these girls is at best non-commital.[16]

Besides these school girls, there are other women in the captivity of these Islamic insurgents whose activities have gone beyond the marginalization of women. In Nigeria today the nefarious activities of these jihadists against women include enforcement of girl-child into early marriage, rape, and assault; denial of rights to freedom and education; and all forms of violation of women and their rights. Never has the Nigerian female-folk bled like in the period between the transition of the federal government from the People's Democratic Party to the ruling All Progressive Congress (2014-2015). In spite of the well-advertised involvement of the developed governments of the United Kingdom, the United States, France, and Israel with the

---

[15] Bringback Our Girls: 276 School Girls Abducted on April 14, 2014, http://www.bringbackourgirls.ng/(Accessed, May 9, 2016)
[16] Maeve Shearlaw Guardian Africa Network, Did #BringBackourgirls Campaign make a difference in Nigeria? http://www.the guardian.com/world/2015/apr/14/Nigeria-bringbackourgirls-campaign-one-year-on.

Nigerian government to obtain the release of these school girls, as of the writing of this project in March, 2016, respite is yet to come.

To add insult to injury, another terrorist group has emerged in Nigeria. It is known as Hausa-Fulani herdsmen. This group of nomads in Nigeria is equally executing terror and horror against families and particularly against women and children. It is now commonplace to watch Nigeria television stations as well as read national newspapers that give vivid accounts of the destruction of lives and property in various parts of Nigeria, particularly in the middle belt and some parts of southern Nigeria. Normally the worst victims of these nefarious activities are children and women. Some of the atrocities committed by these wicked Fulani-Hausa herdsmen are unprintable. They take delight in attacking communities and rural areas, killing the men, raping women, and carrying girls into slavery. They destroy farmlands, cash crops as well as terminate several human communities. They prefer the well-being of their cows, goats, and sheep to the lives of other tribes in Nigeria. Entire communities have been wiped out or fled their homelands and never to return as a result of the menace of these Hausa-Fulani herdsmen. They are usually well equipped with modern military weapons and, worse still, the government of Nigeria is insensitive to the plight of her people.[17]

It is such a hurtful and nagging hydra-headed problem that one is forced to ask whether it is a crime or misfortune to be a woman in Nigeria, nay in early 21st century world. Similar to *Boko Haram*(BH) insurgents are the Islamic State of Iraq and the Syria (ISIS), which is a global form of BH. The ISIS claims authority over all Muslims on the globe and has the goal of Islamizing every mortal on earth. Their female marginalization and destructive policies are similar to those of BH. Recently it went viral in the social media that ISIS is planning to circumcise every female they capture.[18]

---

[17] Ngex, Boko Haram, http://www.ngex.com/nigeria/bokoharam.htm (Accessed May 9, 2015)

[18] Braeme Wood, what is the Islamic State, http://www.the atlantic.com/magazine/archive/2015/03/what-isis-really wants/384980 (Accessed May 9, 2015)

There could be no worse form of women marginalization than the criminal activities of these BK Muslim insurgents in Nigeria and Africa and their Iraqi ISIS group. Perhaps the only comparable partners in crime against humanity in general and women in particular were the slave trade merchants and their accomplices. Africa, Europe, and America conspired to commit heinous crimes against humanity and for over three hundred years. The best brains and most healthy youths of Africa were treated as business commodities across the Atlantic. Only the fittest arrived at the land of the slave masters, while several millions were killed by diseases or their slave masters or thrown into the ocean. Others were tortured, maimed, or starved to death. Among other humiliating experiences, some of the female-folks were raped or served as sex objects for their masters.[19]

It is therefore safer to say that though women marginalization exists in a continuum, it isn't the monopoly of any tribe or tongue, religion, region, season, or section of the globe. The same submission can be made of women empowerment. Women empowerment exists in various societies but perhaps at different degrees.

Furthermore Christianity is no doubt the greatest promoter of women empowerment all over the globe. "For ye are all the children of God by faith in Christ Jesus. For as many of you as have been baptized into Christ have put on Christ. There is neither Jew nor Greek, there is neither bond nor free, there is neither male nor female: for ye are all one in Christ Jesus" (Gal. 3:26-28).

In spite of this clear-cut Christian standard of equality of the genders espoused by the Bible, some Christian groups have continued to promote the policy of women marginalization. Such policies like discriminatory advancement programs, less remuneration, and disregard towards female ministers exist in different degrees in different congregations and creeds. For instance, though there are neither legal nor written policies against the female-folk in my church, there exists some form of women marginalisation. In our leadership

---

[19] Donald R. Wright, 'Slavery in Africa' http://encarta.msn.com 2000 (Accessed May 9, 2016)

cadre in Nigeria, no woman occupies the strategic positions of national, regional, or state overseer. Consequently, this dissertation is a clarion call both to sensitize the church leadership on the need to engage in more empowerment programs for women as well as to carry out such pragmatic programs.

Ranging from the local to international scenes, the need to empower women or create more opportunities for women empowerment grows stronger daily. In Nigeria from the home front, more women are demanding for better healthcare and welfare; from the church and career, they are requesting for equal remuneration and respect with their male counterparts, and in governance, for greater representation and positions of authority.[20] All these point to the need for women empowerment, which is the focus of this study.

How this Project Will Transform a Particular Aspect of this Context

Change may be difficult, but it is the only option for those who desire success. The expected positive changes that would accrue from this project would begin primarily among the leadership and membership of the Charismatic Renewal Ministries, Lagos State, Nigeria. The transformation process will be achieved through the following specific ways:

1. recognition of women's empowerment processes in the Charismatic Renewal Ministries, Lagos State, which is consistent with the basic assumption of Appreciative Inquiry highlighted by Sue Annis "that in every organization, something is working"[21]
2. engaging the church leadership in discussions on how to improve on women empowerment

---

[20] John Okeke, "Stakeholders Demand Improved Women Empowerment in Post Mellinium Development Goals Framework".
http://m.guardian.ng/appointments/stakeholders -demand-improved-women-empowerment-in-post-mdgs-.
[21] Annis, 3.

3. creating a conducive atmosphere for the women to enlighten me the researcher and church leaders on the subjects of marginalization and empowerment
4. developing a Bible study manual as an available resource material which anyone would find as invaluable tool on the subject matter
5. encouraging the women to develop a thrift program among the women that can grow into a store

All these processes are based on the premise that we as a church have the "capacity, expertise, and resources that an alternative future requires".[22]

Summary

This chapter began with the historical background of women marginalization in the African and Nigerian contexts as well as handled current trends and issues on the subject matter. Also, it considered some relevant personal, organizational, and global issues. The chapter ended with a look at how the study will catalyze transformation in some particular areas of the women's lives. In the next chapter, I will be dealing with the crucial issue of literature review.

---

[22] Peter Block, community: The Structure of Belonging. (San Francisco: Berret-Koehler, 2010). Quoted in Evangeline Smith, "An Abode of Abundance: The Positive Outlook of Marginalised Communities" (Term Paper: OVI, Bakke Graduate University 2010)

CHAPTER 3

LITERATURE REVIEW

Introduction

Life is full of paradoxes. Sometimes, it is a contrast between abasement and abundance, darkness and light, ignorance and knowledge. For instance, the subject matters of marginalization and empowerment of women confirm this trend of the contrasting nature of human existence. Marginalization deals with denying the women access and opportunities for leverage or advantages, while empowerment deals with providing leverages.

What is Women Marginalization?

Also referred to as social exclusion, marginalization is a multi-disciplinary terminology that cuts across such academic spheres like, psychology, sociology, economics, education and literature. First used in France, "social exclusion or marginalization refers to denial of fundamental rights and privileges. In particular reference to women, the term deals with systematic blockage or prevention of the feminine gender from enjoying the various rights, opportunities, and resources that are ordinarily provided for them.[1]

Based on this definition, women marginalization is a conscious and deliberate effort and endeavour by the society and her leadership to place women in a degrading second position. According to my experience, marginalization often begins with a mindset and ends up as enacted policies against the feminine gender. Synonyms of women

---

[1] Hilary Silver, "Social Exclusion and Social Solidarity: Three Paradigms," *International Labour Review* 133, no. 5-6 (1994): 531-578.

marginalization include *alienation, disenfranchisement,* and *degradation.*

According to Hilary Silver, "social exclusion is a multidimensional process of progressive social rapture, detaching groups and individuals from social relations and institutions and preventing them from full participation in the normal, normatively prescribed activities of the society in which they live."[2] In relating this definition to women marginalization, we note the following facts.

1. Marginalization is multifaceted.
2. It is progressive (actually degenerative) in the sense that as time goes on, the women or other marginalized groups suffer more incremental loses or denial of rights and privileges.
3. Marginalization can be (and is) institutionalized. In this sense, it becomes a form of systemic evil.

Furthermore, Fredoline Anunobi opines that the marginalization of women in African degenerates from marginalization to gender inequality. She noted that, "although women play a very important role in development, their status in African countries does not reflect their contributions."[3]

These horrendous and sordid attacks against womanhood may not be limited to African society alone. The following statistics confirm the fact that marginalization against women is almost a global event.

1. Thirty-five percent of women, who have been in heterosexual love relationship, report that they have experienced some form of physical or sexual violence.
2. Globally, as many as 38 percent of murders of women are committed by an intimate partners.

---

[2] Hilary Silver, "Social Exclusion: Comparative Analysis of Europe and Middle East Youth Initiative," Mey,i
http://www.meyi.org/uploads/3/2/0/1/32012989/silver_-_social_exclusion-comparative_analysis_of_europe_and_middle_east_youth.pdf (accessed August 1, 2015).
[3] Fredoline Anunobi, "Women and Development in Africa: From Marginalization to Gender Inequality," *African Social Science Review* 2, no. 2 (2002):43

3. Thirty-five percent of women have experienced either physical and/or sexual intimate partner violence or non partner sexual violence.[4]

As a corollary, the United Nations Statistics Division noted that in many parts of the world customs and traditions precondition women to accept abuse as normal.[5] This is very true in Africa.[6]

Degree of Women Marginalization

My observation is that marginalization exists in degree or continuum, ranging from minor mistreatment of women such as verbal insult, abuse, and poor regard, to denial of rights and privileges to the degrading exhibition of physical violence such as vaginal mutilation or circumcision, rape, intimate partner violence, or marital violence and in some occasions, murder. This list is by no means exhaustive. I think that at various times and occasions, women are exposed to different degrees of violation and marginalization. We live in a world where the rich get richer, and the poor get poorer; where the strong get stronger and the weak get weaker.

One of the determinants or indices of societal and human development is the level of protection and provision that is available for marginalized and needy groups such as women and children. In my own view therefore, groups, societies, tribes, and nations that institute the marginalization of women and children are likely to be perceived as underdeveloped, archaic and even barbaric. In pursuit of women empowerment, the United Nations developed seven principles as remedies to end the marginalization of women.

1. the establishment of a high-level corporate leadership for gender-equality
2. equal treatment and respect for both male and female at work

---

[4] World Health Organization, "Violence against Women," http://www.who.int/mediacentre/factsheets/fs239/en/ (accessed July 1, 2015).
[5] United Nations Statistics Division, "Violence against Women," http://unstats.un.org/unsd/demographic/products/Worldswomen/WW2010%20Report_by%20chapter(pdf)/violence%20against%20women.pdf (accessed July 1, 2014).
[6] Kore, Quoted in Ettu Ibid.p.36

3. ensuring the health, safety and well-being of both genders at work
4. promotion of the educational training of women
5. pursuance of enterprise and marketing strategies for the economic empowerment of women
6. promotion of equality of both senders through community development and advocacy
7. regular assessment and publicity report on the progress of gender equality[7]

Conversely, marginalization involves a total reversal of these noble principles.

Women marginalization is a stereotype form of thinking and mindset this is deeply rooted in many societies. Men, particularly, have been implicated as having negative attitudes towards women. Bola Udegbe noted that this prevailing negative masculine attitude towards females can be located in the traditional roles of the two genders, particularly in Africa where such a rigid mindset is measurable in authoritarianism, religious, and conservative attitudes.[8] Based on such an authoritative background, the issue of women marginalization becomes a hydra-headed monster that begins to grow in leaps and bounds as time goes on. Equally, solving the problem would mean returning to handle it from the root.

Marginalization of Women Among Believers

Can believers be engaged in the ugly habit of discriminating against an important cohort of their membership such as the femalefolk? Is the church, the custodian of truth and justice, guilty of perpetuating injustice against the femalefolk? Yet, there is some evidence of female marginalization among believers. "The wife is classified as her husband's property, and so she's listed with the slaves and work animals. There is also a striking omission in this commandment: never

---

[7] United Nations Global Impact, "Endorse the Women's Empowerment Principles," https://www.unglobalcompact.org/take-action/action/womens-principles (accessed August 1, 2015).

[8] I. Bola Udegbe, *Gender and Leadership: Image and Reality* (Ibadan: Vantage Publishers, 1998).

does it say "you shall not covet your neighbor's husband."[9] As uncomfortable as this view is, it shouldn't be easily discountenanced. Rollston strongly opines that the Decalogue promotes the marginalization of women and, of course, he offers the evidence.[10]

A normal religious reaction may be to criticize or ignore Rollston's "outrageous" viewpoint. Some may even classify it as ungodly, but the evidence of women marginalization in the Decalogue remains significant – the wife is classified in the same cluster with the husband's possessions. Again, it was written in recognition of the masculine gender but at the expense of the female.

Furthermore, Rollston adds that the marginalization of women continues in the Book of Proverbs. Solomon, ascribed author of the book of proverbs, addresses sons and neither recognizes nor honors daughters. The famous chapter 31, which recognizes women, was still written in the context that the women bring honor and pleasure to men.

However Pakaluk differs in his evaluation of the Decalogue and the Book of Proverbs. First, Pakaluk notes that Rollston's view was narrow in the evaluation of the Decalogue. The idea of regarding women as the property of their husbands espoused by Rollston cannot be applied to the other commandments such as "Thou shall not commit adultery" and "Thou shall not steal." Pakaluk also opines that Rollston's understanding of the role of women in the Old and New Testaments were shallow and mischievous.[11]

Consistent with Pakaluk's view, that the Bible doesn't support the marginalization of women, there exist examples of women's empowerment both in the Old and New Testaments. The Old Testament describes empowered women like Prophetess Deborah; Miriam; and Zelophehad's daughters, who demanded and received

---

[9] Christopher Rollston, "The Marginalization of Women: A Biblical Value We Don't Like to Talk About," Huffpost Religion, http://www.huffingtonpost.com/christopher-rollston/the-marginalization-of-women-biblical-value-we-dont-like-to-talk-about_b_1833648.html (accessed June 5, 2014).

[10] Ibid.

[11] Michael Pakaluk, "Against Christopher Rollston," http://michaelpakaluk.com/2012/10/14/against-christopher-rollston/ (accessed June 5, 2014).

their father's inheritance. In the New Testament, women were among the 120 disciples who were filled with the Holy Spirit on the day of Pentecost, which is a clear case of spiritual empowerment.

Some, if not the greater majority of the church, is engaged in the ugly practice of women marginalization. "The freedom of women to pray and prophesy in religious gatherings was new that it caused some problems within the church where Jews and Gentiles comingled."[12] It is still a problem today in many churches. This creates the need for this study.

Also Bakke noted the positive Christian influence of his mother's choice in the development of his career and ministry.

Somehow, she created an environment in which everyone was energized, not from fear of punishment or promise of rewards but from a desire to accomplish something positive. She had unbridled confidence in our ability to accomplish the tasks at hand. I can think of a few things she didn't believe we could achieve, even at an early age.[13]

Only an empowered woman could produce empowered giants like the Bakkes. It is very significant to note also that this example of women's empowerment took place more than fifty years ago. Rylko lends a corresponding voice to the issue of women's empowerment among believers when he said, "Women are therefore very important and irreplaceable in the mission of the church. The synod of Bishops in 1987 on the vocation and mission of the laity recommended that it was necessary that the church recognize all the gifts of men and women and put them in practice."[14] There are questions that need to be answered. To what degree does the church implement this written policy? Is it not the evidence of women marginalization that prompted

---

[12] Ettu, *A Christian Response to the Problems of Single Female Adults in the Church* (Owerri, Nigeria: Charismatic Forum Publications, Limited, 2000), 50.

[13] Dennis Bakke, *Joy at Work: A Revolutionary Approach to Fun on the Job* (Seattle, WA: PVG, 2005) 19-20.

[14] Stanislaw Rylko, "Empowerment of Women in the Church and Society," Council for the Laity, Vatican City, Rome, http://www.laici.va/content/dam/laici/documenti/rylko/english/empowerment-of-women.pdf (accessed June 2, 2015).

such a synod and ecclesiastical effort to develop a fair policy for both genders in the church? Even if the policy to recognize and respect women in one denomination is effected, to what extent will it make positive impact in others?

For instance, what is the tangible ecclesiastical authority of women in the Catholic Church? Does the Roman Catholic Church ordain female priests or bishops? Not at all. The Catholic Church allows women into the religious orders of nuns and sisters (as Reverend Sisters) but not into the prestigious order of priesthood. Pope Francis, on his return trip from Brazil, twice noted that the issue of women priesthood in the Roman Catholic Church was a closed one. In his words when the question of possibility of ordaining women priests in the Roman Catholic church was raised, the Pope answered, "The church has spoken and says no... That door is closed."[15]

In the Anglican church, there are different ecclesiastical policies on women's ordination. In the Australian Anglican Church, women were first ordained as deacons in 1986 and as priests in 1992. Currently among the twenty-three dioceses of the Anglican church in Austria, only four (Ballarat, North West Australia, Sydney and The Murray) do not ordain women as priests.[16]

Among the Nigerian Anglican Congregation, the primate of the church most Reverend Nicholas Okoh permits the ordination of women as deacons.[17] Originally in the church of England, the General Synod passed the motion for the ordination of women into priesthood

---

[15] Robert McClory, "Pope Francis and Women's Ordination", National Catholic Reporter, http://ncronline.org/blogs/ncr-today/pope-francis-and-womens-ordination (accessed March 1, 2016).

[16] Anglican Church of Australia, "Are Women Able to Be Priests in the Anglican Church of Australia?"http://www.anglican.org.au/home/about/students/pages/are_women_able _to_be_priests_in_the_anglican_church_of_australia.aspx (accessed March 1, 2016).

[17] Odogwu Emeka Odogwu, "Nigeria: Anglican Archbishop Okays Women's Ordination to the Diaconate," Virtue on Line: The Voice for Global Orthodox Anglicanism, http://www.virtueonline.org/nigeria-anglican-archbishop-okays-womens-ordination-diaconate (accessed March 1, 2016).

in the Anglican church as far back as 1975, and the first woman deacon was ordained in 1987.[18]

The question remains whether these official stands of the Anglican Communion or other churches that favour the spiritual empowerment of women genuinely practice what is written down? Again, do they encourage the congregation to practice gender equality in the church?

I think that generally, the Pentecostal and Charismatic churches tend to favour female spiritual empowerment more than the orthodox mainline churches. This is based on the fact that the doctrines, practices, and lifestyles of the former are based more on the teachings of Christ and the New Testament. Given that the Holy Spirit is the Spirit of liberty and freedom, Pentecostal and Charismatic churches authorities would be better placed to champion and exemplify women empowerment. In some occasions this is true, while at other times, there is much left to be desired.

If … women are (no) less capable than men of piety, zeal, learning and whatever else seems necessary for the (ministry), then why… should the church not draw on the huge reserves which could pour into the priesthood if women were here, as in so many professions, put on the same footing with men.[19]

I believe the truth is that women should be encouraged and allowed to be ordained. The optimistic summary of the issue is that though marginalization of women may be evident among believers, there is a conscious effort to empower the female-folk in the contemporary church.

Marginalization of Women in the Charismatic Renewal Ministries, Lagos State.

From my observation, *culture shock* is the term that describes the response of some male leaders in the Charismatic Renewal Ministries

---

[18] The Church of England, "The Women Priests Debate," https://www.churchofengland.org/our-views/women-bishops/the-women-priests-debate.aspx (accessed March 1, 2016).

[19] Paul K. Jewett, *The Ordination of Women* (Grand Rapids: Wm. B. Eerdmans Publishing Co,14, 1980) Quoted in Sheri R. , "Pentecostal Women in Ministry: Where Do We Go from Here?" *Cyberjournal for Pentecostal-Charismatic Research,* http://www.pctii.org/cyberj/cyberj1/ben.html (accessed March 1, 2016).

when the issue of women marginalization was raised. They expressed surprise and amazement. Culture shock has been described as "that feeling of loss of bearing and distress which characterizes those who are uprooted from their familiar environment".[20] The reason for this culture shock is obvious – these men experienced the strange feelings of amazement because they thought that the Charismatic Renewal Ministries neither supports nor practices any form of marginalization of women. The culture shock feeling was heightened by specific examples of women marginalization.

1. Insignificant percentage ratio of female to male representation in top leadership position.
2. Less ministerial assignment allotted to females.
3. Unequal regard and respect for male and female ordained ministers.

However, there is neither an oral authority nor written document that initiates and promotes such measures of women marginalization in the church. Specifically, the constitution of the Charismatic Renewal Ministries Incorporated is neutral on the issue of gender marginalization. "The ministry may ordain any of its members who is duly qualified into any of her pastoral or ministerial office. The General Core Group shall have the final say on whether or not any one is qualified for ordination"[21]

The relevant question here is Does the written document correlate with the church practice? Does the ideal correspond with the real? Are the standards of the Charismatic Renewal Ministries on the issue of gender equality on ordination matters, consistent with the practice? Sometimes yes, and at other times they vary, and it is on these issues of inconsistency that the problem of women marginalization in the church rests.

---

[20] Geddes & Grosset, *Webster's Universal Dictionary & Thesaurus* (New York: David Dale House, 2005). 134.

[21] Charismatic Renewal Ministries, *The Constitution of Charismatic Renewal Ministries* (Owerri, Nigeria: Charismatic Forum Publication, 2004).

Barbara Elliot noted a similar case of female marginalization: Mother Teresa of Calcutta who needed to prove the authenticity of her calling before her male dominated superiors.

When Teresa asked to be released from the convent to go onto the streets, she was denied permission. She was told to say nothing and go back and pray, which she did obediently. As she waited, the outcomes of what she was to do become clearer. She asked again, but her superiors in the church still doubted the authenticity of her call. Once again, she went back in obedience to pray. Again, permission was not granted.[22]

There are two ways of considering the case of Mother Teresa and her superiors. First is that such a test of character was necessary both for prospective male and female ministers. It was a test of patience, perseverance, and ultimately love. Both male and female ministers of the gospel should be prepared to undergo tests and trials.

Another viewpoint is that Mother Teresa's case was one of female marginalization because her superiors were predominantly males –the Catholic priests and bishops who were neither female nor understood the travails of femininity. I believe that an important aspect of the experience one may not neglect was that a fair, representation of females among Mother Teresa's superiors would equally have produced a better and faster evaluation of her character and ministry.

Life is dynamic and change is the only constant variable. The issue of women's empowerment also is improving. Ray Bakke R. and Jon Sharpe confirmed this improvement when they noted that

Women have emerged as the signs of hope in most of the cities we know about. It seems that the more violent a community, the more necessary it is that women lead. We knew that women cut right through to the core of problems. Male church leaders often threaten emasculated men in such communities. Unless we learn to follow

---

[22] Barbara J. Elliott, *Street Saints: Renewing America's Cities* (Philadelphia: Templeton Foundation Press, 2004).

these women, we might as well write off these communities for evangelism or church ministry.[23]

One major lesson from these two authors postulations is that the church needs to empower more women because these women are strategically relevant and invaluable for the advancement of the kingdom business. Women play major roles both in the evangelization of the community as well as church leadership. The Charismatic Renewal Ministries cannot but follow the trend of women empowerment. Moreover, as a strong advocate of servant leadership, the church can only tread the path of women empowerment.[24]

What is Women Empowerment?

There are various explanations of women empowerment. A common focus of all of them is that women empowerment involves processes and program that enable women to maximize the potentials, which will ultimately enhance self esteem and worth. For instance, the United Nations Population Information Network noted that there are five components of women empowerment.

1. A restored sense of feminine worth.
2. Ability to have as well as determine choice.
3. Women's right to have access, opportunities and resources.
4. Women's right to have the power to control their own lives.
5. The ability to influence the direction of social change to achieve social and economic order.[25]

In summary, women empowerment involves all the processes that are focused on the pursuit of achieving wholesome, healthy, and fulfilled lives for women. One asks, is this an issue the women should pursue or leave in the hands of their male counterpart? I think it should

---

[23] Raymond J. Bakke and Jon Sharpe, *Street Signs: A New Direction in Urban Ministry* (Birmingham, AL: New Hope Publishers, 2006), 144.

[24] Cosmas Ilechukwu, *The Church of His Vision* (Owerri, Nigeria: Cannif Trust Ltd., 2002).

[25] United Nations, "Guidelines on Women's Empowerment," United Nations Population Information Network (POPIN), http://www.un.org/popin/unfpa/taskforce/guide/iatfwemp.gdl.html (accessed July 1, 2014).

a collaborative venture. Patience Itai Hove collaborates this view in her work that advocates for women leadership in the Zimbabwean society.[26]

Furthermore, women empowerment is considered as the increasing psychological, social, political, economic, and spiritual strength of women, which ultimately leads to the development of personal confidence in personal abilities.[27] My stand is that the development of personal confidence in one's abilities is very fundamental not only for success in life but as well in attaining fulfillment and satisfaction. Attainment of healthy self-esteem and worth will likely enhance success in life endeavours.

I strongly believe that due to a long history of degradation and marginalization, many women are prone to psychological distresses, which may manifest as inferiority feelings, deep feelings of inadequacy, discouragement, depression or in some cases suicidal thoughts may occur. "These emotional and sometimes mental disturbances among women can be classified as anxiety, phobia, and personality disorders".[28] Therefore empowerment will reverse this terrible trend of marginalizing among women as well as deliver them from unnecessary psychological and physiological hazards.

Scope of Women Empowerment Opportunities

In writing about Appreciative Inquiry, Watkins, Mohr, and Kelly say, "Our use of the term "appreciative" emphasizes the idea that when something increases in value, it "appreciates." Therefore, "appreciative inquiry" is inquiry that focuses on the generative and life-giving forces in the system that are the things we want to increase. By "inquiry" we

---

[26] Hove, xv.

[27] Stephanie Ouellette, "Definition: Women Empowerment," Self Growth, http://www.selfgrowth.com/articles/Articles_Women_Empowerment.html (accessed August 1, 2015).

[28] Emma Enekwechi, "Abnormal Behaviour and Behaviour Change" *A Handbook of Psychology: An African Orientation* eds, Isidore E, Eyo& Hyacinth Obi-Keguna (Nsukka, Nigeria: Great AP Express Publishers, 2004), 434.

mean the process of seeking to understand through asking questions."[29]

The relevance of this quotation is in relation to masculine and societal worldview and perception about women. Effective empowerment must begin from the point of appreciating the worth and role of women. As men and the larger society begin to do so (or engage in more) of such positive ideas and actions, the women will experience the release of greater potentials as well as achieve greater goals. Some of the available empowerment opportunities for women exist in the spheres of education, the economy, marriage, careers, spirituality and leadership.

Educational Empowerment

Beginning with the issue of education, women should be given equal opportunities with men to acquire quality education. The discrimination against the girl-child should stop. The education of women is basic and central to achievement of women empowerment. Like the axiom goes, if you think education is costly, try ignorance. Illiteracy and ignorance are prices too dear to pay in a lifetime and more dangerously in the present technologically advancing world.

The formal and non-formal education systems would need to be considered. It would be important to analyze the gender content and to ascertain the manner in which it is addressed or not addressed in the educational system. On the basis of analysis, curriculum, changes would need to be brought about.[30]

I therefore submit that education for women should be formal but should extend beyond the four walls of the classroom. It is crucial in the sense that such an educational curriculum prepares them to engage in a self-improvement program. Also crucial is that such educational

---

[29] Jane Magruder Watkins, Bernard J. Mohr, and Ralph Kelly, *Appreciative Inquiry: Change at the Speed of Imagination* (San Francisco: Pfeiffer, 2011), 22.
[30] Carolyn Medel-Anonuevo, "Women, Education and Empowerment: Pathways Towards Autonomy," UNESCO Institute of Education, Hamburg, Germany http://unesdoc.unesco.org/images/0010/001006/100662e.pdf (accessed July 1, 2015).

programs for women should be relevant and useful to their gender roles.

Some of the advantages of literacy among women include the realization of family hygiene and quality health, good child spacing, access to balanced diet, improved marital relationship for the couple, provision of a conducive home atmosphere for the children's continuous education as well as attainment of personal fulfillment. Furthermore providing quality education for women offers them opportunities to compete equitably with their male counterparts from any part of the globe in the spheres of career, business or governance. A common axiom has it that the education of a male benefits his immediate circle of influence, while the education of a woman results in the education of several generations. This statement underscores the need to empower women academically.

Economic Empowerment

Closely related to educational empowerment of women is the issue of economic or financial leverage. What are the available opportunities for the economic empowerment of women today in sub-Saharan Africa and Nigeria?

In a general sense, one may assume that the positive forces of globalization and technological advancement have balanced the geographical and gender inequalities of economic oppression. Yet this may be a far cry from the true situation. For instance, geographically and developmentally, African women are still marginalized. As a corollary, Dejene notes, that "women's lack of access to productive resources in Africa is a serious economic problem for the continent. Denying working women the opportunity to own and inherit property has serious implications on the productivity and income of households."[31]

---

[31] Yeshiareg Dejene, "Promoting Women's Economic Empowerment in Africa," AFDB,
http://www.afdb.org/fileadmin/uploads/afdb/Documents/Knowledge/25040341-FR-DRAFT-DEJENE.9-15-07DOC.PDF (accessed July 1, 2015).

I believe articulating and implementing an effective economic empowerment program for African women would attract a lot of advantages to the family and society at large. Taking cognizance of the diverse personalities of women, their ages, educational levels, financial needs and availability of funds, these women can be gainfully engaged in blue-collar and white-collar jobs. Others can be involved in micro and skill acquisition businesses. Some of the advantages that will accrue from the economic empowerment of women include provision of improved feeding; healthy home environments; funding of children's educations; and a significant change of status, which will be evident in improved standard of living. Consequently, economic empowerment of women in Africa is a laudable venture that needs to be pursued with vigor.

Marital Empowerment

"In Nigeria as in other developing African countries, women have inferior social status to men - a situation foisted and encouraged by age-long traditional system."[32] The idea of empowering women in their homes and marriages involves change of mindset from viewing them as liabilities to assets; from regarding women as mere housewives, whose place is only in the home front (or kitchen), to regarding them as co-partners in progress; from seeing a woman as her husband's property to accepting her as an equal.

I believe the right beginning point to ensure that women are empowered in the home is for men to appreciate that marriage is a partnership and complementary union of two adults. Each gender has an appropriate role to play. Very fundamentally, both are naturally equipped to play their distinct roles. It is a case of division of labour based on gifting, abilities, and specialization. Consequently, neither should lord it over the other but recognize and encourage the other to be the best he or she was created to be. Anything contrary to this approach of the marriage union will result to marginalization which portends problems in the home and the larger society.

---

[32] Women Entrepreneurs Association of Nigeria, ed., *Women Anti-Poverty Project* (Lagos, Nigeria: Ivory Agency Limited, 2009), 27.

Consequently, such marginalization signs like verbal and physical violence and psychological and physiological oppressive tendencies against women will become history. As a basic form of women empowerment, gender equality in the home should be conscientiously pursued because lack of it may likely ruin the efforts to achieve empowerment in other spheres or endeavours.

Spiritual Empowerment

Perhaps the area of spiritual development is the most crucial sphere where women should be empowered, given the fact that religious leaders by the nature of their spiritual enlightenment and education will show a greater understanding, empathy and concern towards women. My observation is that it isn't always the case.

In the course of researching for this project I discovered that, many Christian leaders are involved in several programs of women marginalization. "Examples of such religious marginalization against women include pursuing policies such as restriction of women's ecclesiastical authority and administration of sacraments, discrimination against women in terms of remuneration and honorarium"[33]. In many churches, in spite of the natural and spiritual endowments of a woman, she can never be allowed to preach in a local church assembly. She is restricted to minister only to children, youths, or women only. I regard such restrictive policy on women ministry as a form of marginalization. Qualified and gifted women should be allowed to minister to both men and women.

Spiritual women empowerment is necessary for the advancement of the family, organizations, and the society at large. In specific terms empowering women spiritually would involve the following.

1. Accepting and affirming their equal status with men in the church.
2. Proffering them equal opportunities with their male counterparts in every sphere or endeavour of life.
3. Authorizing women to attain any and all levels of ecclesiastical hierarchy.

---

[33] Robert McClory, "Pope Francis and Women's Ordination", National Catholic Reporter. Ibid.

4. Eliminating every policy that promotes economic marginalization and psychological oppression of women. Instead the church replaces these with policies which enhance the empowerment of women.

These spiritual empowerment policies that the church deliberately engages in will enhance the lives of both the membership and leadership. Again, it will encourage the fulfillment of the vision of the church. Women are known to be significant positive stakeholders in the church business.[34]

Leadership

Allowing and encouraging women to take up leadership positions in every aspect of life's endeavors is an undeniable evidence of empowering them. "It is not biblically, theologically, or culturally correct for one gender to rule over another, nor to be ruled by another. As a result, there is need to raise the female to top leadership positions by creating equal opportunities."[35]

Yet in real life, women are constantly denied equal opportunities to assume leadership positions in various areas of life in the African society by the male dominated leadership. The prevailing male mindset is that women are the weaker vessel; they are too emotional to handle complex rational decisions; Or women cannot cope with the intricacies and intrigues, difficulties, and dangers of assuming top leadership positions in various spheres of human endeavour. Yet the positive result the Nigerian society and church receive from a few of the women who have broken the barrier of male marginalization and ventured into top management positions prove that women can be excellent and exceptional leaders. Nigerian government and church leadership need to encourage more women to assume leadership positions in the various aspects of human endeavour.

This policy of raising women to the position of equality with men should cut across every institution of our society such as family, community life, education, business, careers, government, and church.

---

[34] Bakke and Sharpe, 144.
[35] Ibid., xiv.

In my opinion, the result would be phenomenal. It will provoke healing, restoration, and greater advancement for the entire human race.

Women's Empowerment in the Church

I begin this section with an insightful statement by James Dobson.

If I could write a prescription for the women of the world, I would provide each one of them with a healthy dose of self-esteem and personal worth (taken three times a day until the symptoms disappear) I have no doubt that this is their greatest need ... if women felt genuinely respected in their role as wives and mothers, they would not need to abandon it for something better.[36]

I have more questions need to be asked. What is the root cause of this inferiority complex in women? Who determines the quality or degree of a woman's self-esteem? The answer to both questions, I think, is the organized society and church as led by men. When will men allow women or assist them to become the best God created them to be?

Consequently, and in agreement with Hove, any effort to achieve genuine empowerment among women must involve collaboration between the two genders.[37] Of a necessity, this study will engage such collaboration of some church male leaders and women.

Some of the specific ways the church empowers women include the following.

1. Equitable administration of sacraments.
2. Supporting women education at all levels as against the traditional African religion and Islamic policies of promoting illiteracy among women.
3. Advocating for better healthy and conducive living conditions for women.

---

[36] James Dobson, "On Low Self-Esteem Among Women" Quoted in Joyce Landorf Heatherley, *The Fragrance of Beauty* (Wheaton,:Victor Books, 1973), 75.
[37] Hove, xv. Ibid.

4. Providing some level of economic empowerment for the needy and poor, common in some churches.

Consistent with the idea of the church empowering women, Scorsone noted, "The church, throughout its long history, has been peopled with empowered women-military leaders, judges, chatelaines and controllers of property – many of whom are now revered as saints. In addition, the church has had a long history of involvement with the education of women and girls."[38]

Though the idea of favouring women empowerment was the picture in the Catholic Church, it truly represents the position of the church on women empowerment. Catholic, Anglican, Pentecostals, Protestants, or any other subsection of the church believes as well as practices some level of women empowerment.

Also in agreement with this view, Baur made this relevant input.

The following year, the Pastoral Commission of the Congregation for Evangelization, after wide consultation, suggested the following women's activities, based on their natural potentialities: their specific educational role in Catechism, schools, pastoral institutes, minor and even major seminaries, preparation for all sacraments. Sisters presiding over the Sunday liturgy without priest... Much remains to be done before the immense resources of women are fully used for the Kingdom of God.[39]

The last statement is both interesting and instructive. Yes, much needs to be done in spite of the various empowerment policies before the church can fully tap the resources of the women-folk. The church should continue to improve in her empowerment programs towards the female-folk.

---

[38] Suzanne Scorsone, "The Church Has Defended Women's Rights for 2,000 Years" (lecture, UN Commission on the Status of Women, March 3, 1998), http://www.cco.caltech.edu/~nmcenter/women-cp/church_empowers_women.html (accessed July 1, 2015)).

[39] John Baur, *2000 Years of Christianity in Africa: An African History, 62-1992* (Nairobi, Kenya: Paulines, 2005), 480.

Women Empowerment in the Charismatic Renewal Ministries.

In his ground breaking book, *The Church of His Vision*, Ilechukwu, the General Overseer of the Charismatic Renewal Ministries Incorporated, rightly noted,

We must uphold the truth that men and women have equal opportunities to use the gifts God has given them to serve one another and the world as the spirit leads every one. It is never the intention of God for man to be alone and work alone. In the beginning God made them male and female and commissioned them to steward creation on His behalf.[40]

From the foregoing one can understand that the Charismatic Renewal Ministries supports and engages in women empowerment. The various practical ways the Charismatic Renewal Ministries empowers women include the following.

1. Championing the education of the girl child.
2. Advocating for the welfare as well as sound health of women.
3. Encouraging women to participate in theological training.
4. Recognition of their gifts and abilities.
5. Encouraging women to assume leadership positions in the various cadres of ecclesiastical echelon.
6. Defending the sacredness of marriage as well as protecting women from the disadvantageous traditional cultural influences.

Ilechukwu sums ups the reality of women empowerment in the Charismatic Renewal Ministries when he said, "If a woman can be filled with the Holy Spirit, and be endowed with spiritual gifts, then she has divine authority to exercise such gifts in the church of His vision. Service in the church must be gift based. Whoever God has gifted in any area is the person He has called a function in that area."[41]

As positive and potent as these statements are, there still remains opportunity for improvement in the issue of women empowerment in the Charismatic Renewal Ministries. This study recognizes the positive policies the church is already implementing and seeks to

---

[40] Ilechukwu, *The church of His Vision*, 410.
[41] Ibid., 418.

improve on them. As noted by of Baur, "Much remains to be done before the immense resources of women are fully used for the Kingdom of God."[42]

Summary

This chapter focused on the review of relevant literature on women marginalization and empowerment. It considered the scope of both issues and considered the incidence of women empowerment in the church. The next chapter provided the biblical and theological themes of the study.

---

[42] Baur, 2000 years of Christianity in Africa, 480.

CHAPTER 4

BIBLICAL AND THEOLOGICAL THEMES

Introduction

This study is designed to empower Charismatic Women by employing the instrument of Appreciative Inquiry. In Chapter 1, the statement of problem and objectives of the study were discussed. Also the problem questions and hypothesis were stated. Chapter 2 dealt with the context of the problem, and, chapter three outlined the review of literature. This chapter addresses the following biblical and theological themes related to the topic of empowering women: stewardship, discipleship, leadership, family, and careers.

These five themes relate to the subject of women empowerment in diverse ways. In the first place, they are integral aspects of women's life and empowerment. Women function as stewards of divine resources, are involved in discipleship, leadership, family, and career issues.

Again, a positive approach to these issues in relation to the lives of women in the church will enhance their empowerment. On the contrary, neglecting to handle or to exclude women from the crucial issues of stewardship, discipleship, leadership, family life and as well as developing their careers will only amount to marginalization. Therefore these five subthemes are relevant, current, and invaluable for enhancing women empowerment in the church.

Stewardship

An easily misunderstood word, *stewardship* is one of the themes related to the topic of women empowerment in the Church. I think that few of the erroneous interpretations given to stewardship include the care for mundane affairs, taking care of the economy, business, or an assignment reserved for the less privileged. However, stewardship is more than these mundane tasks. Banks and Stevens noted that "The term denotes a more comprehensive view of the Christian life affecting time, work, leisure, talents, money, and the state of one's soul and care of the environment. The Greek word for *steward* (*oikonomos*, from which we get our word *economy*) means one who manages a household."[1]

Thus, stewardship is a comprehensive biblical term that has a close tie with the subject of this project topic – empowerment. Stewardship includes discovery, development, and deployment of these various resources as they affect both male and female-folks. In the Parable of Talents (Matt. 25:14-30), Jesus never made distinction between male and female stewards. Should the Church be involved in discriminating between the genders in the issues of discovery, development, and reward of resources? Shouldn't the Church follow the Master's example?

Stewardship can be defined as "the willingness to be accountable for the well-being of the larger organization by operating in service rather than control of those around us. Stated simply, stewardship is practicing accountability without control or compliance."[2]

Productivity or fruitfulness is a major concern of stewardship. Jesus copiously illustrates this lesson of fruitfulness in John 15. He called His followers to bear fruit (v.2), He prunes them to bear more fruit (v.2) and to grow into bearing much fruit (v.8). He wants that fruit to abide or remain (v.16).

Consequently, unproductivity or barrenness is an abnormal condition in the life of a steward. The question now is Does God permit women to be unfruitful in His vineyard? Is there any empirical evidence to buttress the fact that women are excluded from Jesus demand for

---

[1] Robert J. Banks and R. Paul Stevens, eds., *The Complete Book of Everyday Christianity: An A-to-Z Guide to Following Christ in Every Aspect of Life* (Downers Grove, IL: InterVarsity Press, 2007), 962.

[2] Peter Block, *Stewardship: Choosing Service over Self-Interest* (San Francisco: Berrett-Koehler Publishers, 1993), xx.

fruitfulness in Ministry? Not at all. Ilechukwu aptly captures the important role of women in stewardship when he noted that

What role women should play in the church would depend on what gifts God has bestowed on any of them. It does not depend on the established tradition or what the malefolk feel about women in ministry. There is a great need of humility here, to acknowledge what God is doing among us irrespective of the vessel of operation, whether woman or man. If it is possible for women to be endowed with spiritual gifts then they must play a role in the life and ministry of the church.[3]

The lessons from this quotation are explicit. The stewardship gift of women goes beyond the walls of the church and reaches out to other life endeavours such as business, governance, education, and community life. Consequently society needs to recognize, encourage, and help them to develop and utilize these abilities to serve God and humanity. Accountability is one of the basic requirements of stewardship. It means that the Benefactor will demand that the beneficiaries who received the resources should explain how they managed them. Very remarkably, every mortal came into this world naked and empty and will return in the same manner. However in the lifetime of every mortal, human beings receive numerous resources that everyone must give account of.

"Every good gift and every perfect gift is from above, and comes down from the Father of lights, with whom there is no variation or shadow of turning" (James1:17). In the Old Testament there are see biblical examples of stewardship. Eve was Adam's partner in the stewardship of the Garden (Gen. 2:15). If not, she would have been exempted in bearing the consequences of disobeying God (Gen. 3:16-19). They were partners in blessing and curses, joys and sorrow, sowing and reaping.

Sarah was Abraham's co-labourer in bringing to pass God's promise of receiving Isaac. She played major roles in influencing Abraham to marry Hagar as well as divorce her. In fact, when Abraham was

---

[3] Ilechukwu, *The Church of His vision,* Ibid., 414.

44

thinking of rejecting Sarah's advice to send away Hagar, the bondwoman, and Ismael her son. God instructed Abraham to listen to (obey) his wife. "But God said to Abraham, 'Do not let it be displeasing in your sight because of the lad or because of your bondwoman. Whatever Sarah has said to you, listen to her voice; for in Isaac your seed shall be called" (Gen. 21:12). This Abrahamic biblical example is a very difficult test for every husband (including Christian men) to pass. God was telling Abraham to listen or obey his wife, which demonstrates God's instructions in the context of stewarding God's purpose for a godly home. Abraham and Sarah were already setting the standard for New Testament families. Paul instructed Christian husbands and wives to "submit to one another in the fear of God" (Eph. 5:21).

In the New Testament, Aquila and Priscilla were Paul's co-labourers. Priscilla was an excellent steward of bivocational Christian ministry because she was involved both in the Gospel and market place business of tent-making (Acts 18). The gifts or resources God bestowed on males are neither superior nor more important to the human society than those of females. In other words, every gift, ability, or resource is significant, and depending on such variables like time, history, need, culture, and population, the relevance or demand of each of these gifts or resources may vary. God will demand account of these gifts and, therefore, they should not be neglected.

Discipleship

Let me begin this section with a quotation from I. Howard Marshall et all

A disciple (from Lat. Discipulus; pupil; learner; corresponding to GK. Mathētes from manthano; to learn) is basically the pupil of a teacher. In the Gk world, philosophers were likewise surrounded by their pupils. Since pupils often adopted the distinctive teaching of their masters, the word came to signify the adherent of a particular outlook in religion or philosophy.[4]

Consequently, discipleship is the process of making or producing a disciple. It has to do with commitment to learn or discipline oneself or to acquire knowledge. For the Christian, it means learning to become like Jesus. As a lifelong process, there will always be room for improvement.

In connection with the subject of the thesis, which is women empowerment in the Church, it is necessary that the teaching and learning curriculum for members of the local assembly should include topics and issues on marginalization and empowerment. Right from the children's class, the church leadership should begin to discourage any form of discrimination against the femalefolk or any gender at all.

Jesus the Lord and Master would have the Church to honor and value everybody. The scriptural standard is to reject every form of discrimination against people, which means receive and honor all people.

"For as many of you as have been baptized into Christ have put on Christ. There is neither bond nor free, there is neither male nor female: for ye are all one in Christ Jesus" (Gal. 3:27-28). This issue of gender equality illustrated in Jesus' specification of the characteristics of disciples. Ettu rightly captures the cost of discipleship as enunciated by Jesus when he said,

Discipleship-making must be to the extent of transforming the worldview of the Christianized person'. All Christians in the Bible, in church history, and in our time, whom God used or is using as His instruments who made significant contributions to the practical advancement of Christianity... were or are men and women who

---

[4] I. Howard Marshall et al., *New Bible Dictionary* (Leicester, England: InterVarsity Press, 1996), 277.

surrendered or have surrendered their lives totally to the Lord; men and women whose hearts were or are transformed for Jesus; Discipleship.[5]

From Ettu's useful input on discipleship I note that God doesn't discriminate between male and female. Both male and female disciples of Jesus must experience transformation of life. Mbajiorgu provides further insight into the discussion on discipleship.

Discipleship is not a state of passive defeatism; a state of being quiet and bearing it because you cannot beat them and you cannot join them. Discipleship is also not popular religious piety neither is it the opium of the masses. Discipleship is an aggressive, attacking and conquering crusade. It is an active life supported by a heavenly divine life that achieves the divine purposes.[6]

Such lifestyle cannot be exclusive to males alone. God supports both females and males to attain their optimum levels of development as well as achieve their utmost in life. Consequently, neither human beings nor any system should marginalize women from fulfilling their divine purposes.

The 120 disciples who were filled with the Holy Ghost on the day of Pentecost were made up of both men and women.

And when they had entered, they went up into the upper room where they were staying: Peter, James, John and Andrew; Philip and Thomas; Bartholomew and Matthew; James the son of Alphaeus and Simon the Zealot; and Judas the son of James. These all continued with one accord in prayer and supplication with the women and Mary the mother of Jesus and His brothers. (Acts 1:13, 14)

By this Jesus' and early church example of raising both male and female disciples, the standard is set for the New Testament church. Actually, examples of true female disciples abound in the early church, such as Dorcas, the charitable disciple in Joppa who was raised from the dead (Acts 18:24-26); and Lydia the business woman of Thyatira

---

[5] Lawrence O. Ettu, *A Case for Authentic Christian Morality in Africa* (Owerri, Nigeria: Charismatic Forum Publications, 2010), 5.

[6] Magnus Mbajiorgu, *The Making of a Disciple* (Lagos, Nigeria: Change Publications, 2005),19.

who Paul baptized (Acts 16:14, 15). Added to this significant number of women disciples are the women who were among the 120 disciples in the upper room on the day of Pentecost.

Consequently, one concludes that God doesn't discriminate between the genders in the crucial issue of discipleship making. In fact, no christian can neither become or do their best without becoming disciples. Discipleship actually empowers both males and females to function maximally.

Equality of the genders and respect of all peoples are the targets of this thesis. An early and adequate, continuous and conscientious discipleship program in the Church along the sound doctrine of Christ for both genders will achieve this target.

Leadership

What is leadership? How does it relate to the subject of women empowerment? Beginning with the definition of *leadership*, the connection to empowerment becomes obvious. "Leadership is influence, the ability of one to influence others, to follow his or her leader. Famous leaders have always known this."[7]

Remarkably, this definition of *leadership* as influence has been popularized by John Maxwell, who erroneously most people think is the originator of this idea. As a significant influence on others, Leadership can be tailored towards positive or negative impact. Consequently, the leadership of the Church can be geared towards empowering women instead of marginalizing them. This empowerment will be best demonstrated in word and action. Peter said, "Feed the flock of God which is among you taking the oversight thereof, not by constraint, but willingly; not for filthy lucre, but of a ready mind; Neither as being lords over God's heritage, but being examples to the flocks" (1Pet. 5:2, 3).

True leadership is by example. It is similar to Jesus' form of servant leadership. Leadership is equipping others to achieve their God-given

---

[7] J. Oswald Sanders, *Spiritual Leadership: Principles of Excellence for Every Believer* (Chicago: Moody Publishers, 2007), 27.

vision.[8] When the leadership of the Church champions women empowerment, the entire Church will likely follow in the same step. "The most important single ingredients in the formula of success is knowing how to get along with people."[9] Many Church leadership personalities and teams in Africa need to get acquainted with getting along with the femalefolk. We need to understand the cry of the downtrodden and marginalized significant group in the churches and society.

The relevant question here is, Can women take up effective leadership positions in the church and society? Particularly in Africa and Nigeria, can Christian women be expected and encouraged to lead? If not, why not? If yes, at what level?

In Kenya, Catherine Dolan argues that the post colonial state has deliberately exploited biblically based gender roles to keep women trapped in an arduous household production system. She describes a typical village gathering at which the chief quoted biblical texts to emphasize the importance of female submission. The women remained silent through the sermons exalting motherhood, domesticity and Christianity.[10]

No doubt, this Kenyan odious example is typical of most African societies. Yet, the trend is changing positively in favor of encouraging women leadership in the church.

On the day of Pentecost, both men and women who made up the one hundred and twenty disciples that waited in the upper room, were all baptized in the Spirit and all spoke in other tongues as the Spirit gave them utterance. God did not discriminate between male and female in the great Pentecostat outpouring. He obviously does not discriminate

---

[8] Adeola Olukemi Ilechukwu, "Mentoring as a Tool for Raising Servant Leaders" (diss., Bakke Graduate University, 2011).
[9] Theodore Roosevelt "On Successful Relationship" quoted in John C. Maxwell, *The 21 Indispensable Qualities of a Leader: Becoming the Person That People Will Want to Follow* (Nashville: T. Nelson, 1999),103.
[10] Catherine Dolan "The Good wife" quoted in Philip Jenkins, *The New Faces of Christianity: Believing the Bible in the Global South* (New York: Oxford University Press, 2006),161.

between them in their exercise of spiritual gifts for the work of the ministry.[11]

This is appropriate. Women in African churches are beginning to experience some significant form of empowerment. The church has begun to share ecclesiastical powers with women. Many Pentecostal and Charismatic Churches now ordain women. Jenkins notes that

Questions about female leadership matter, since women have long been prominent in many of the independent churches. Africa has a vibrant tradition of women prophets, including such fiery leaders such as Alice Lenshina,… Naturally, then, even churches that officially cite St. Paul's alleged rules of exclusion find room for female authority, by citing such biblical leaders as Deborah.[12]

Particularly in the Charismatic Renewal Ministries, women are in the leadership positions from the local church to state, regional to national. Also have some of them we ordained ministers. Out of the eight ministers who occupy the highest ecclesiastical position in the Charismatic Renewal Ministries, referred to as the General Core Group, one of them is a woman. It will be desirable to have more women involved in the leadership of I Charismatic Renewal Ministries at the national and state levels. One hopes that the policy of empowering women in the area of leadership should increase in the church as well as affect other spheres of life in African societies.

Family Life

In the contemporary world where norms and values attract less attention, one may ask, what is a family? What is the biblical standard of family life? What does the Scripture say about the roles of males and females in the home? Is it cohabitation of two youths, same sex adults, or that of a human being and an animal? Furthermore, is it a relationship between an adult male and several females or vice versa?

---

[11] Ilechukwu, *Church of His vision*, Ibid, 414.

[12] Philip Jenkins, The New faces of Christianity: Believing the Bible in the Global South (New York: Oxford University Press, 2006), 168.

However, in the context of this study, a family refers to the enduring relationship of an adult male and female with or without the blessing of children. Also it is in agreement with the biblical standard that stipulates that a man should leave his parents and be joined to his wife (Gen. 2:24). The case of single parenting can also be referred to as a family.

Consequently, women play major roles in both marriage and family live. Solomon captures the crucial role of women in home building when he said, "Every wise woman builds her house but a foolish one pulls it down with her hands" Prov. 14:1. Women play the significant roles of nurturers, care-givers, companions, motivators, shock-absorbers, mothers and lovers, and sometimes breadwinners in the family.

I believe that family life is generally accepted as the safe heaven as well as the advantageous place of the femalefolk. It is practically impossible to think of a complete and healthy family life without the woman. Right from childhood, in most African societies, the girl-child is wired to assume a leadership position in the home. During play sessions, she chooses to cook instead of shooting with guns as her male sibling or friend would naturally do. She is more likely to be interested in home affairs in her early years and in such related activities such as marriage and care-giving.

Actually, I believe that men and women have specific roles in the home. The home is like a company or organization where the man is the chairman while the woman is the managing director. The man's major roles are to cast the vision of the home as well as become the major provider of the resources for the smooth running and success of the home. The woman complements all the good efforts of the man as well as sees to the daily running of the home. She is the manager, home-maker, and builder. She is the burden-bearer and the center of the home. Also I believe that by nature, the woman is a life-giver and therefore, has capacity to nurture and protect every investment entrusted into her care. In some occasions the woman plays both the role of being the breadwinner as well as complements the man. Such women need to be complimented and appreciated rather than criticized or marginalized. It must be the light of the understanding of the crucial roles of women in the family that the writer of Proverbs 31 said, "Who can find a virtous wife? For her worth is far above rubies" (Prov. 31:10). This appreciation of women is appropriate.

If therefore this same female is maltreated, maligned, and marginalized at the home front, where she is supposed to play significant and productive roles, it becomes a case of double tragedy. Truly, some women are facing such traumatic and terrible situations at home. From case studies of verbal abuse and assault, spousal violence has become the norm instead of the exception in many homes.[13] This trend goes beyond Africa. For instance one Austrian source confirms that "the vast majority of dangerous, abusive and violent behavior that occurs in the privacy of people's home is committed by men against women."[14]

Instead of marginalizing women at the home front or in any sphere at all, the men should join hands with the former to empower the women. The special and significant roles of the female folk should be nurtured and celebrated "The woman is therefore someone who renders support and thus compliments the efforts of another."[15] This view is a confirmation of the Scripture that says, "And the LORD God said, it is not good that a man should be alone; I will make him a helper comparable to him" (Gen. 2:18). Equally, she needs to be affirmed and shown affection so that the home can achieve the noble purpose for which it was set up. In the Charismatic Renewal Ministries, most women are enjoying their family lives. The two factors responsible for this positive trend are genuine conversion as well attainment of basic education of most of the members. Also, both genders have a regular

---

[13] Passy Amaraegbu, "Understanding Spousal Violence," *Successful Family Magazine Beta Edition Centre for Marriage and Family Stability*, (2012), 11-13.

[14] Domestic Violence Prevention Centre, "Domestic Violence Statistics," http://www.domesticviolence.com.au/pages/domestic-violence-statistics.php (accessed September 1, 2014).

[15] Joseph Mensah, *The Woman of the Spirit* (Owerri, Nigeria: Charismatic Forum Publications, 2013),13.

monthly meeting at the local assembly where training is conducted on the issues of Christian home and marriage. Yet, there are some families in Charismatic Renewal Ministries, Lagos State, Nigeria that have difficulties in coping with the Christian standard of family life. This negative trend creates the need for the study.

Women like men, are made in the image of God and should be respected and empowered to achieve their God-given goals.

Then God said, let us make man in Our image, according to our likeness; let them have dominion over the fish of the sea, over the birds of the air, and over the cattle, over all the earth and over every creeping thing that creep on the earth. So God created man in His own image: In the image of God He created him; male and female He created them. (Gen. 1:26, 27)

Marriage offers every couple a great opportunity to lay down a solid foundation for the empowerment of both genders.

Career Life

Should women be involved in developing their careers or be content with the traditional role of being homemakers? Should Christian women be actively involved in working, or doing business outside their homes? Should Charismatic women be involved in developing their careers outside their home-front zone? The answer is in the affirmative. The reason is that women are equally endowed like men, and like men can acquire adequate and specialized skills to pursue virtually any career they set their minds on.

The Scriptures, provide examples of such professional career women as Deborah the judge (Judges 4:1-5); Rachel the farmer (she shepherded Laban's flock) (Gen. 29:6); Miriam, a significant woman leader (Exod. 15:20, 21); Jael, the great warrior who killed general Sisera of Canaan (Judges 4:17-24); Priscilla, the astute teacher of the Word (Acts 18:24-26); the evangelist woman of Samaria (John 4:5-29); Mary, the first preacher of the resurrection (John 20:1-18); and others. One might say that there are always exception to every rule but the fact is that factors like societal stereotypes, maternal responsibilities and marginalization by the societies mostly ruled by men have been denying the femalefolk the opportunity of pursuing their God-given careers.[16]

Men condone and take pleasure in emphasizing traditional behavioural roles of women, thus reinforcing the belief that the workplace is men's territory. To males, particularly in male-dominated occupations, the presence of women threatens the solidarity of the work culture and eradicates the trust and camaraderie among them. Such attitudes tend to impede upward movement opportunities for women.[17]

I personally believe that it is the duty of the church to teach by words and example that women have equal opportunities in the marketplace. African church leaders and congregation should rise to this occasion.

Faith Oyedepo noted that most women are embarrassed that the society doesn't expect them to work.[18] Both in the church and society women have the mind to work. The excuse of using child bearing to deny them access to developing their careers and lives is unrealistic. Before marriage and after the years of child bearing, the female-folk can be engaged in active development and deployment of their abilities to pursue various careers virtually to any level of attainment. Creating such opportunities for women to develop and pursue their careers is a veritable tool for their empowerment. The federal government of Nigeria is making some significant effort along this line. For example, in the former regime of President Jonathan, women occupied such sensitive positions in our federal government as, Minister of Finance and Head of Joint Economic Team, Ministers of Petroleum, Water Resources, Foreign affairs (Junior) and Communications. These positions were based on merit and not sentiments because these women are all specialists in their different fields of endeavour. One hopes that

---

[16] Regina Eya, "Adulthood and Ageing" Quoted in, *A Handbook of Psychology: An African Orientation* (Nsukka, Nigeria. Great AP EXPRESS PUBLISHERS LIMITED, 2004), 247.

[17] Udegbe, 6.

[18] Faith A. Odeydepo, *The Effective Minister's Wife* (Canaan Land Ota, Nigeria: Dominion Publishing House, 2008).

subsequent governments will sustain and improve on this positive trend of women empowerment in public service.

It is remarkable that both in the Old and New Testaments, women were significantly involved in career ventures. For instance, Rebekah, the wife of Isaac, was both physically and mentally strong. In the contemporary world, she would be referred to as a woman who possessed beauty and brain. Abraham's chief servant who was charged with the responsibility of choosing a wife for Isaac prayed for divine direction to choose the right woman.

And it happened that before he had finished speaking, that behold, Rebekah, who was born to Bethel son of Milcah, the wife of Nahor, Abraham's brother, came out with her pitcher on her shoulder. Now the young woman was very beautiful to behold, a virgin: no man had known her. And she went down to the well, filled her pitcher and came up. (Gen. 24:15, 16)

Rebekah went ahead and filled the pitchers of water, which satisfied the thirst of the company of Abraham's servants as well as their camels (Gen. 24:17-22). This demonstration of hospitality, strength, and expertise earned Rebekah the position of first lady in Isaac home. The question is after marriage should such a wonderful lady be rendered redundant?

A significant example is that of the great evangelist woman of Samaria. A remarkable story of transformation from prostitution to preaching the Good News. This single woman courageously brought an entire community to the feet of the Master (John. 4:1-22).

In the Charismatic Renewal Ministries, women are encouraged as well as challenged to develop their careers. Most of us in the Charismatic Renewal Ministries, are graduates who met Christ on campus. Both men and women originally had the mind to pursue and develop different career paths. Therefore getting saved and married only encouraged us to fulfill each other's earlier goal of pursuing a fruitful career path.

Of course, I cannot say that everybody in Charismatic Renewal Ministries fits into this picture whereby women are particularly encouraged to pursue their careers. There exist some cases where women are denied this noble opportunity, and I am hoping that such situations will be remedied with continuous enlightenment.

Summary

The focus of this chapter was to provide both biblical and theological bases for the issue of women empowerment in the church. It considered the five relevant themes: stewardship, discipleship, leadership, family life, and career life. Chapter 5 focuses on the methodology used to carry out the study.

CHAPTER 5

METHODS OF RESEARCH

Introduction

Providing more qualitative and quantitative leverages for the female-folk of Charismatic Renewal Ministries, Lagos State is the focus of this study. From chapters 1 to 4 the background of the various relevant variables related to the study were outlined. This chapter 5 describes the methodology used in carrying out the study and the following subsections are incorporated within: research design, population and sampling procedures, size, data collection as well as procedure of analysis.

The purpose of this study is to explore possible and better ways of empowering Charismatic Renewal Ministries Women in Lagos State, Nigeria. The study considered the various factors that lead to the marginalization of the female-folk as well as the past and present levels of women empowerment in the church. Furthermore, the project will consider the role of the male folk in empowering women.

Research Design

Consistent with the topic of the study, the data gathering method of choice was Appreciative Inquiry, which is a form of qualitative design. Consistent with Hove's viewpoint, qualitative research is interested in investigating the qualitative value of human behavior as well as the motive of behavior.[1] It is regarded as the appropriate research design for this study because the study deals with individual belief systems, values, perceptions as well as mindsets. These personal stereotypes develop overtime due to consistent thought patterns and actions. These

---

[1] Hove, Ibid, 110.

fixed ways of thinking develop into the reality of life and therefore influence people's behaviors. Consistent with Sue Annis'postulation, "AI is based on the positive principle that some things work well in every group or organization."[2] Consequently, the questionnaire and interview followed the Appreciative Inquiry format. The questions were addressed to two major groups, namely, the women and male dominant leaders of the church.

Research Population and Sampling

Charismatic Renewal Ministries Lagos State 1 and 2 is comprised of twenty-one branches and six zones. The population of the female-folk of the two arms (States 1&2) is about 1500. There were two categories of participants, namely the Charismatic Women and their male leaders drawn from the two branches. These participants were chosen through purposeful sampling. Sensing recommends this form of sampling as being appropriate for the Doctor of Ministry dissertation.[3] Justification for purposeful sampling also includes the fact that these subjects had a high level of awareness and interest on the matter at hand (in this case women empowerment in the church). Sensing provides other reasons for the choice of purposeful sampling that are appropriate to this study. The reasons are subjects who "represent a certain opinion, confirming or disconfirming cases," people who represent the typical case," and suggested by lead interviewees.[4]

Sample Size

From each of the two churches in the Lagos State branch of Charismatic Renewal Ministries, a minimum of four participants (four women and six male leaders) of the target research sample was used

---

[2] Sue Annis, Hammond, Appreciative Inquiry (Bend: Thin Book Publishing Company, 1998), 3.
[3] Tim Sensing, *Qualitative Research: A Multi-Methods Approach to Projects for Doctor of Ministry Theses* (Eugene, OR: Wipf & Stock Pub, 2011), 83.
[4] Ibid., 83.

for the study. Effort was made to draw a balance between the male and female participants. However there were more females because the study primarily was focused on them. The participants were identified from the leadership list of the two churches. Four male subjects were selected from Dominion and Surulere churches and six each from the two churches for a total of eight males and twelve females.

Table 1 shows the male and female sample respondents of the Appreciative Inquiry interview of the participants in the study.

Table 1. Distribution of Participants Interviewed

S/N	Church/Zones	Males	Females	Total Respondents
1	Dominion	4	6	10
2	Surulere	4	6	10
	Total Respondents	8	12	20

These participants were drawn from the leadership list of male and female leaders of the two churches namely, Dominion and Holy Ghost Centers in Lagos State, Nigeria. The total number of participants was twenty, eight males (four from each church) and twelve females (six from each church).

Table 2 shows the number of respondents to the questionnaire from the two Charismatic Church Centers, namely Dominion and Surulere. The number of males and females was each, for total of eighty participants.

Table 2. Distribution of Questionnaire

S/N	CHURCH/ZONES	MALES	FEMALES	TOTAL RESPONDENTS
1	Dominion	20	20	40
2	Surulere	20	20	40
	Total Respondents	40	40	80

The Charismatic Women were married women, ages 30 to 55, with a basic level of education of the West African Certificate of Education (WAEC), while the leaders were men whose level of Christian leadership in Charismatic Renewal Ministries Lagos State ranged from church unit or departmental leaders to ordained center pastors. The purpose of including both genders was to draw a balance.

Research Instruments

Questionnaires and interviews were the research instruments that were used to gather data for the study. Effort was made to tailor them to fit the Appreciate Inquiry model.

Furthermore, in the process of developing these Appreciative Inquiry questionnaires and interviews, effort was made to maintain the standards of objectivity, validity, and reliability. Both questionnaires and interviews were pretested and corrected to achieve standardization. The questionnaires involved both structured and unstructured formats.

Questionnaires

The questionnaires were distributed by hand to the Charismatic male leaders and women members. One of the main challenges of questionnaires and surveys is low rate of response by participants. At some other times, the problem was lack of understanding or even confusion with some of the items. These problems were handled or at least brought to a minimum by my direct involvement as the researcher in administering the questionnaires.

The questionnaires did have some advantages that have enhanced the result of the study. The advantages included anonymity, saving time and they were less expensive to produce. Also, the questionnaires afforded me a great opportunity to interact and assess the participant.

Interviews

The study relied rely more on an unstructured than structured format. The interviews complemented the result of the questionnaires because as noted by Sensing, they facilitated deeper probing which revealed the interior lives of the participants.[5]

Data Collection

Data collection followed the previously described format for the research instruments used in this study. The first stage was to conduct Appreciative Inquiry interviews with both the selected Charismatic male leaders and the females. The second stage involved the distribution, collection, and collation of the two different questionnaires.

Appointments were secured for the interview sessions. Research assistants were trained in conducting the interviews as well as administering questionnaires.

Data Processing

After data collection and collation, responses were sorted and converted to the format which tallied with the questions. Data processing consisted of questionnaire coding, data cleaning, and entry. The SPSS format was used to collate the questionnaire, while data from interviews were collected based on the relevant and logical themes. Two forms of statistical analysis were used, first, the statistical package for Social Science (SPSS) for the general evaluation of all participants to analyze the data. Secondly, a two-way Analysis of Variance (ANOVA) was used to analyze the data. The rationale for this choice of statistics was based on the fact that I tested for two variables at two different levels namely, gender (male/female) and level of empowerment (poor/high).

Intervention Strategy

The 4-D Cycle of Appreciative Inquiry is the most appropriate intervention approach for the study. According to Sensing this intervention approach involves the four stages of "Discovery, Dream,

---

[5] Ibid., 103.

Design, and Destiny."[6] They are also referred to as "appreciating, envisioning, constructing, and sustaining"[7] simultaneously. Each of these stages is important in completing the cycle. At the discovery stage I considered the already existing evidences and proofs of women empowerment in the Charismatic Renewal Ministries, Lagos State. The focus of the dream stage was what might be possible about further empowerment of these women. At the design stage, I discussed what should be done to actualize greater women's empowerment in the church, and at the destiny stage, I focused on actual innovative processes and strategies of women empowerment in the church.

Specific Steps to Implement Intervention Stage

The intervention approach of choice was the 4-D cycle, which is represented by the four stages of discovery, dream, design and destiny. Let me describe these in some details.

Discovery Stage

According to Sensing this initial stage is focused on "what gives life to the organization."[8] What is the organization already doing well? What signs of hope are identifiable in the organization?

This discovery stage was handled with care and wisdom so as to act as a springboard for more successful inquiry. My effort at this initial stage of A.I. intervention was to unveil and reveal the existing or present advantages, strengths, and positive aspects of the organization. Questions for my project included the following.

1. What are the identifiable ways the Charismatic Renewal Ministries, empowers women?

2. Enumerate some of the practical ways the Charismatic Renewal Ministries empowers women.

---

[6] Ibid., 170.

[7] Ibid., 171

[8] Cooperrider, David, L. and Diana Whitney, "Appreciative Inquiry: collaborating for change. Edited by Peggy Holman and Tom Davane: (San Francisco: Berrett-Kochler, 1999) Quoted in Sensing, 172.

Dream Stage

The focus of this second stage was imagining the possibilities that could become reality. This stage is a mental exercise that can (and should) be expressed concretely in writing. Sensing referred to this dream stage as the envisioning impact stage.[9] In relation to my project, the relevant questions included the following.

1. What mental imageries or pictures do you hold about an empowered Charismatic Woman-resourceful, satisfied, and joyful?
2. To what extent can the church empower the women – partially or maximally?

A seminar on women empowerment was introduced at this stage of the intervention with further planning conducted in the design stage.

Design Stage

This third stage focused on what should be. According to Sensing, it is the dialogue or construction stage.[10] It may easily be confused with the dream stage. The distinguishing factor is that while the dream stage is the desirable future, the design stage is the reality that emerges out of dialogue and discussion. It is a test of reality. Questions included the following.

1. What should be some practical ways and means of empowering Charismatic Women?
2. Given the peculiarity of the Church, potentials and problems, strengths and weakness, what are the real ways the church leadership can engage in women empowerment?

This design stage of the intervention was rounded off with considering further development of the second part of the seminar on women empowerment, which was held in November 2015 and focused on some practical steps of women empowerment.

---

[9] Sensing, 171.
[10] Ibid., 171.

Destiny Stage

Also referred to as the sustaining stage, this last one focused on what will be. The relevant questions included the following.

1. What women empowerment programs would the church engage or embark on to improve the status of Charismatic women?
2. What percentage of the church's annual budget will the leadership commit to women empowerment projects and programs for the next five to ten years?
3. What leadership strategy or program would the church set up to sustain the program of women empowerment?

Economic empowerment of women is a relevant choice of empowerment for this study. At this stage, I made a strong case for the women to engage in cooperative thrift business.

Evaluation Methods

One of the ways to evaluate the data collected for the study was to cross-check similar questions and answers proffered by the women and the leaders. Also these questionnaires and interviews were administered to many other women and leaders as a way of determining internal consistency. Also, I employed the service of an independent expert as well as provided a personal interpretation of the questionnaire in order to achieve the validity of the data because according to Sensing validity and reliability are fundamental essentials of an authentic research.[11]

Conclusion

The focus of this chapter was to outline the research methodology. Qualitative research design was the chosen approach, while the instruments were questionnaires and interviews. Appreciative Inquiry (AI) was the appropriate intervention model. Also the research population, sample, instruments, data collection, and analysis

---

[11] Ibid., 171.

procedures were presented in the chapter 5. The next chapter is the analysis of findings and recommendations.

CHAPTER 6

ANALYSIS OF FINDINGS AND RECOMMENDATIONS

Introduction

Chapter 5 was a presentation of the methodology of the study, while this chapter focuses on as well as discusses the results and findings of the study. Consequently the analysis is guided by the research questions. Also, the connection between research findings and literature review will be made. Therefore, recommendations from the study will be made on the basis of the findings.

This study focused on Appreciative Inquiry as a strategy for empowering women in Charismatic Renewal Ministries, Lagos State, Nigeria. The main design was a descriptive survey that employed the use of structured interview and questionnaires.

There were two types of questionnaires for male and female leaders, while the same interview format was used for both male and female participants. A total of eighty questionnaires were distributed and all were returned. In the interview section, a total of twenty leaders participated: eight males church leaders and twelve female church leaders. Their responses are presented in the following sections.

Data Collected – Matrix Of Findings

Data showing the eighty completed questionnaires sent out to the two Charismatic Churches in Lagos State Nigeria are presented in tables 3 and 4. A set of twenty questions were given to the women and another twenty to the men in the two different branches of the church. The SPSS system was used to analyze the data collected, and all the findings were tabulated.

Table 3 shows the results of the female responses to the questionnaire, which was aimed at revealing the level of women empowerment from the

66

feminine point of view. There were twenty questions. Some of the major areas of women empowerment this questionnaire focuses on are acceptability of women leadership by both genders, equality of ministerial remuneration, and freedom to exercise spiritual gifts in the church, plus others.

Table 3. Female responses to questionnaire

S/N	Questions	Holy Ghost Center					Dominion Centre				
		HGC	SA	AA	WA	NAA	DC	SA	AA	WA	NAA
1	In our church both males and females enjoy a cordial relationship.	20	12	4	1		20	15	1		
2	As a female leader I feel safe in church.	20	16				20	14	1		
3	As a female leader I enjoy my status and role.	20	10	5		1	20	12	4		1
4	I enjoy the support of other female leaders.	20	3	6	3	8	20	4	5	3	7
5	Women leaders out number male leaders in our church.	20	1	10	4	3	20	2	12		3
6	Women are better leaders than men.	20	1	6	5	7	20		4	6	8
7	As a female leader my supervisors listens more to me than my male colleagues.	20	1	6	5	7	20	2	7	3	8
8	As a female leader my subordinates cooperate more with me than my male colleagues.	20	2	8	3	6	20	3	9	4	4

#	Statement										
9	Generally female leaders are preferred to males in our church.	20	1	5	1	11	20		5	1	12
10	Husbands accept and affirm their wives.	20	6	6	3	1	20	7	5	4	1
11	Families with females leaders enjoy more harmony than those with males.	20	7	12	2	6	20	6	11		2
12	As a female leader I enjoy equal financial income with male colleagues.	20	4	6	4	5	20	3	5	5	5
13	I enjoy a sense of harmony among male leaders.	20	11	5	1		20	13	4	2	
14	I enjoy harmony among fellow female leaders.	20	14	6	1		20	12	4	2	
15	I would gladly be a member of a church led by a woman.	20	11	6	1		20	10	5	2	
16	I will vote a fellow woman into leadership position.	20	12	6			20	14	6		
17	I will gladly obey women leadership.	20	12	2	1		20	13	1	2	
18	I freely exercise my spiritual gifts in the church.	20	17	3		16	20	1			
19	There is no limitation to my career development.	20	13	2	1	1	20	10	3	1	1
20	I can freely express my opinion in our	20	12	3	1		20	13	2		

	church.										
	Total	400	166	107	37	70	400	154	95	55	52

KEY
SA – STRONGLY AGREE
AA – AVERAGELY AGREE
WA – WEAKLY AGREE
NAA – NOT AT ALL

Table 4 presents the results of the male questionnaire, which focused on highlighting male leadership attitudes and opinions on women empowerment. These twenty questions covered such women empowerment issues as male approval of female leadership, education, and financial empowerment.

Table 4. Male Questionnaire

S/N	Questions	Holy Ghost Cantre					Dominion Centre				
		HGC	NAA	S	A	AW	DC	NAA	S	A	AW
1	Many women in our church are appointed to lead.	20		3	7	10	20		2	9	9
2	It is normal for women in our church to lead groups constituting of both males and females.	20		2	10	8	20		4	12	4
3	Males in our church approve of female leadership.	20		2	6	12	20		1	7	11
4	Male in our church are delighted with female leadership.	20			9	11	20			12	8
5	Most women in our church are educated.	20		1	4	15	20		2	11	7
6	Our church encourages women education.	20			6	14	20			5	15
7	Males in our church approve of women education.	20			3	17	20			4	16
8	Our church has a program/project centered on encouraging women education.	20			8	12	20		1	6	13
9	Most women in our church are rich.	20		10	9	1	20		6	12	2

No	Statement											
10	Our church encourages women to be economically independent.	20		2	4	14	20			5	15
11	Males in our church encourage women to be economically independent.	20			4	16	20		2	4	14
12	Our church leadership has a program for empowering women economically.	20		2	10	8	20		6	10	4
13	Every woman in our church enjoys her marriage.	20		1	15	4	20		2	13	5
14	Our church encourages women to enjoy their marriage.	20			3	17	20			2	18
15	Husbands in our church work diligently so that their wives can enjoy their marriage.	20		2	12	6	20		1	13	6
16	Our church has a marriage counseling programme geared towards helping wives to enjoy their homes.	20		2	2	16	20			2	18
17	Every woman in our church is mentally sound.	20			13	7	20		4	12	4
18	Our church encourages the mental health of women.	20			4	16	20			5	15
19	Men in our church facilitate the mental health/development of women.	20		1	4	15	20		1	3	16
20	Our church deliberately encourages the mental development of women	20		1	7	12	20			6	14
	Total	400		29	154	248	400			32	154	214

KEY

NAA – NOT AT ALL

S – SCARELY

A – AVERAGELY

AW – ALWAYS

Matrix of Interviews

Table 5

Table 5 is the matrix of interviews of the male and female leaders of the two churches, namely Holy Ghost and Dominion. The centre pastors of both churches as well as male and female leaders who occupied important positions participated in the Appreciation Inquiry (AI) interview. These interview sessions took place in the church halls and office.

Table 5. Interview Matrix

Name	Gender	Position
Holy Ghost Church		
1. Pharm. Marcel Udebuani	M	Center Pastor
2. Pastor Ignatius Ihejirika	M	State
3. Mr. Yinka Fesobi	M	Administrator
4. Mr. Nse Essien	M	Associate Pastor
5. Pharm. Chimezie Amaraegbu	F	Associate Pastor
6. Mrs. Ngozi Omojiade	F	Pastor in-charge
7. Mrs. Chibuzor Osazee	F	of women
8. Mrs. Annie Adobe	F	Children
9. Mrs. Florence Isaac	F	Associate Pastor
10. Mrs. Uche Udebuani	F	Media Unit
		Music Unit
		Music Unit
		Evangelism Unit
Dominion Church		
1. Pastor Sunny Orere	M	Center Pastor
2. Mr. Daniel Enilama	M	Associate Pastor
3. Mr. Leonard Okolo	M	Men
4. Mr. Yemisi	M	Associate Pastor
5. Mrs. Patricia	F	Evangelism
6. Mrs. Ngozi Leonard Okolo	F	Associate Pastor
7. Miss. Patricia Adewunmi	F	Associate Pastor
8. Mrs. Camela Ogbumudia	F	Music Unit
9. Mrs. Babara Chibuisi	F	Associate Pastor
10. Mrs. Jane Orere	F	Children Dept.
		Sanctuary
		Cleaning Dept.
		Ushering Unit.
		Associate Pastor

Table 6 is the matrix of means of a two-way Analysis of Variance of the Holy Ghost male and female leaders on the measures of women empowerment. It was a follow-up test of the questionnaire.

Table 6. Matrix of means of 2 way Analysis of Variance (ANOVA) of Holy Ghost Church Male and Female

	A	B	C	D	ROW TOTAL	ROW MEAN
Male	-	30	154	240	424	106
Female	62	37	106	155	360	90
Column Total	62	67	260	395	Grand Total	796
Column Mean	31	335	130	197.5	Grand Mean	98

Table 7 is the matrix of a means of a two-way Analysis of Variance of the Dominion Centre male and female leaders on the measures of women empowerment.

Table 7. Matrix of means of 2 way Analysis of Variance (ANOVA) of Dominion Centre Male and Female

	A	B	C	D	ROW TOTAL	ROW MEAN
Male	-	32	154	214	400	100
Female	52	35	94	154	335	83.75
Column Total	52	67	244	368	Grand Total	735
Column Table	26	33.5	122	184	Grand Mean	183.75

The women's empowerment seminar was carried out in the two churches in November 2015, while the evaluation was in January 2016. Table 8 is the score of the male and female participants of the two churches (Holy Ghost and Dominion Centers) in the project evaluation seminar, which tested four specific areas.

Table 8. Scores on Evaluation of Project Intervention/Seminar
Dominion Centre
Question 1

S/N	Male Score	Percentage	Female Score	Percentage
P	1	10%	1	10%
F	3	30%	5	50%
G	5	50%	2	10%
E	1	10%	2	10%

Question 2

N	1	10%	0	0%

L	3	30%	4	40%
A	5	50%	6	60%
S	1	10%	0	0%

Question 3

P	1	10%	2	20%
F	2	20%	2	20%
G	6	60%	6	60%
E	1	10%	0	0%

Question 4

N	0	0%	0	0%
S	0	0%	2	20%
O	6	60%	2	20%
A	4	40%	6	60%

Holy Ghost Church

Question 1

S/N	Male Score	Percentage	Female Score	Percentage
P	0	0%	0	0%
F	3	30%	4	40%
G	4	40%	5	50%
E	3	30%	1	10%

Question 2

N	0	0%	0	0%
L	1	10%	1	10%
A	3	40%	5	50%
S	5	50%	4	40%

Question 3

P	0	0%	0	0%
F	1	10%	1	10%
G	9	90%	7	70%
E	0	0%	2	20%

Question 4

N	0	0%	0	0%
S	0	0%	2	20%
O	2	20%	2	20%
A	8	80%	6	60%

Data Analysis

Holy Ghost Church Charismatic Female Leaders (Surulere)

Table 3 is a matrix of results of the questionnaire administered to female leaders in two of the branches of Charismatic Renewal Ministries in Lagos State, Nigeria as shown in appendix A. Table 4 is a matrix of the questionnaire administered to male leaders in the same two branches of Charismatic Church as shown in appendix B. Also Table 5 is a matrix of interviews carried out on both genders of the two churches as shown in appendix C. Table 6 and 7 are the matrix of two-way ANOVA carried out on Holy Ghost church and Dominion church males and females, respectively. Table 8 is the matrix of the Evaluation result carried out on Dominion center and Holy Ghost church as shown in appendix E.

The analysis of the questionnaires indicates a general acceptance and affirmation of females as significant members of the church. The female leader of the church in the Charismatic Renewal Ministries Surulere, Lagos Nigeria, has regard for themselves. In practical terms the church leadership approves the development of women in diverse spheres of life such as education, career, economic pursuits as well as in the area of ministry.

Furthermore, and maybe fundamentally too, there is no church legislation against any form of women marginalization. Constitutionally and legally there is every opportunity for women to develop and grow in different aspects of their lives and ministries. However this near perfect picture of women empowerment in the Surulere Holy Ghost Church isn't always the true picture of the issue at hand. It is the ideal.

The reality on ground is that there still exists some level of women marginalization in the Charismatic Renewal Ministries, Surulere, Lagos. The result of the questionnaires indicates that 41.5 percent of females believed that the church practiced empowerment. This percentage believed and consented to be proponents of women empowerment. One notes this positive impact as aanindication of improvement. The other side of the coin is why does the larger population of women, 58.5 percent, in the Surulere church believe that the church leadership position on women empowerment is weak? This result is recorded in spite of the official church position of a favourable and strong position on women empowerment.

Some of the proofs of women marginalization in the Surulere Charismatic Church included a few homes where wives were left alone to handle childcare and therefore prevented them from working in their careers, and in some cases a husband's negligence of wives' health occasioned by ignorance. This form of negligence of wives' health may be the reason there is a variance between the opinions of male (62 percent) and females (41.5 percent) on the subject of women empowerment in Surulere Church. The position of most women in Africa as the direct victims of marginalization positions them to offer first class evidence and eye witness accounts of the ugly incident of marginalization. It is a case of he (she) who wears the shoe knows where it pinches most. Taking into account extreme cases of emotionalism (such as under or overreporting of women marginalization), the fact remains that in most parts of sub-Saharan Africa, the male dominated leadership in the church and other organizations need significant improvement in the issue of women empowerment.

The differences between male and female responses to appreciation of women empowerment was further subjected to two-way analysis of Variance (ANOVA), and the result indicated a significant difference $F(3,19) =1.92$, $P<.05$. The degree of variance in the level of the two genders appreciation of women empowerment can be understood along the line of their different constitutions, perceptions and functions. In my own opinion, men are generally objective, while women are subjective. Men are predominantly mental, while women tend to be emotionally inclined. Furthermore, I think that this result could be influenced by experiential bais whereby because women are directly the victims of marginalization, they have a higher propensity to be oversensitive to their needs while their male counterparts (the perpetrators of female marginalization) may be colour-blind towards issues of women empowerment. The result of the Appreciative Inquiry of women empowerment in the Charismatic Church Surulere indicated that 80 percent of them appreciated women empowerment.

Both men and women who were interviewed agreed to a very large extent (80 percent) that men and women in the church complemented each other. The women noted that their husbands as well as the male leaders in the church respected and held women in high regard. What then was responsible for the incidences of women marginalization that arose at different times in the home and church?

Cultural norms and practices constituted a form of carry-over from the African society to the church. The transformational power of the gospel was still at work in the lives of such males who were struggling between yielding to the Gospel or to continue to practice male chauvinism, which is strongly part of the African culture.

Particularly for the women, the seminar on women empowerment was a significant contribution towards attaining the goal of appreciation of women. They felt that the seminar/Bible study should have come earlier in the church than now. However, they concluded that it was better to be late than never. Most of them demanded and received their own copies of the seminar as a reference document.

Holy Ghost Charismatic Male Leaders (Surulere)

The result of the questionnaire administered to the male leaders in the Holy Ghost Church, Surulere indicated that 62 percent of them believed in women empowerment. Actually these male leaders should have performed better because of some relevant reasons. First the exemplary lifestyle of the top leadership of the ministry/church on the issue of women empowerment. The General Overseer of Charismatic Renewal Ministries is a strong advocate as well as practitioner of women empowerment. Also the consistent exposure of these male leaders to relevant New Testament materials and teaching on women empowerment is meant to assist them attain a greater degree of appreciation of women. As significantly positive as this result is, what accounts for the 38 percent of male leaders who didn't believe in women empowerment in the Surulere church? As an urban area with a lot of enlightenment and exposure for residents to civilization and modern technology, I expected that all these enabling factors would positively impact women empowerment. Perhaps it is a case of traditions persisting for a long period. The transformation of the malefolk in the church is a gradual process. Further subjection of the result of the male leaders response to women empowerment to two-way analysis of Variance (ANOVA) indicated a significant difference: $F(3,19)=1.92$, $P<.05$.

Most of the males interviewed were of the opinion that women are reluctant to use the opportunities of leadership provided for them in the church. What then could be the reason why for this untoward response of women to leadership in the church?

I discovered that a long history of women marginalization in the society and even church contributed to the problem of women shying away from leadership responsibility. The degree of socio-economic development of the family was also contributory. Many families in the Surulere axis of Lagos are middle class. The predominant picture of the family is that of a career or business father (husband) and a house-caring mother (wife). Women who are allowed to pursue their careers normally employ a house-keeper or are able to attract the help of an extended family member.

I observed that, most Christian women leaders unconsciously translated their followership in the area of career (instead of leadership) position to the church. Of course, many are not happy with their roles as perpetual assistants and helpers instead of taking the leadership position.

Contrary to the opinion that women don't like taking the lead in the church, all the women indicated that they experienced satisfaction and fulfillment when the church leadership gave them opportunities to lead such as during the annual Women's Week, preaching in the youth as well as adult services. The question then was, Couldn't the frequency of women leadership of programmes and projects in the church be expanded to include more for the former? Both genders agreed that the programmes and projects involving women should be expanded but 60 percent of the men noted that women as weaker vessels should not be stretched and overstressed with the onerous task of leadership. The male leadership opined that it was right for them to exhibit gender sensitivity by reducing the responsibility of women. They reminded me that women were the weaker vessels and therefore shouldn't be over burdened with leadership responsibility as men.

Furthermore 100 percent of males opined that there was room for improvement in the degree of appreciation and women empowerment in the church. This empowerment encompasses every aspect of the women's life as demonstrated in the seminar.

The impact of the seminar on women empowerment was significant and positive. Both genders were receptive towards the study as well as desirous that it should be incorporated into the Bible study programme of the church.

Dominion Charismatic Women Leaders (Egbe)

Egbe, the location of Charismatic Renewal Ministries, Dominion Centre differs from Surulere, Holy Ghost church not only in terms of geographical location but also in terms of the socio-economy level. The former is a suburban, while the latter is entirely urban. Yet, most of the challenges faced by women in both locations of Charismatic Renewal Ministries are similar. The responses of the female leaders revealed that 38.5 percent of them believed that Charismatic Renewal Ministries practiced women empowerment. These women provide such proofs of women empowerment in the church like encouraging women to improve their education, provision of welfare for indigent families, and economic empowerment in terms of providing funds to assist small scale business women.

The women did point out some areas of challenge the predominantly church male leadership experienced in difficulty of empowering women. For instance, while many women would be glad to be members of a church led by a woman, it isn't so with their male counterpart. Most male leaders may not mind belonging to a church with female associate pastors but do oppose a church where the senior or only pastor is a woman. Such negative factors like discrimination against church female leadership, economic impoverishment of women, and a general lack of care (due to poverty) of the women may account for the significant percentage (61.5 percent) of women who opined that the Dominion Centre Church leadership didn't substantiate their claim to women empowerment.

When the different responses of the male and female leaders of Dominion Centre to appreciation of women empowerment was subjected to two-way analysis of Variance (ANOVA), the result revealed a significant differences of $F(3,19)=2.09, P<.05$. I note that the difference for females was lower than males (38.5 percent versus 52.8 percent). Women reported a lower level of appreciation for empowerment in the church, most probably because the issue of marginalization and empowerment engage their lives and personalities more directly their male counterparts.

Moreover the introduction of the seminar on women empowerment was a watershed event. The women welcomed the study with open hearts and hands. It was like an efficacious drug that would handle the disease called women marginalization. One notable area that the women desired church male leadership appreciation is economic empowerment. The target is to start a women thrift or cooperative business that will handle to a large extent the problem of poverty among the women. The men were cooperative with the women in this area.

From the Appreciative Inquiry interview, 100 percent of women observed that the New Testament teaching of the Bible has impacted positively on male negative perception of women in their church. This excellent positive report is inconsistent with the earlier report of 38.5 percent the women's observation of women empowerment in the Dominion Center. One way to explain this discrepancy is that the women consider the two issues of development of New Testament culture and women empowerment as distinct issues. Both men and women believe that through consistent teaching effort coupled with exemplary living, more men will come to appreciate women as well as become significantly involved in empowering them.

Dominion Charismatic Men Leaders (Egbe)

One of the peculiarities of Egbe, the location of Charismatic Renewal Ministries Dominion Centre, is that it is suburban. The Christian male leaders of the Charismatic Renewal Ministries Dominion Centre who believe in women empowerment was 32.8 percent. The result is against the 52.8 percent of those in the urban area of Surulere.

Consequently it can be stated that the level of socioeconomic development of any community or city affects the degree of masculine appreciation of the feminine gender as well as the level of women empowerment. As perceived, the negative impact of African culture on women is stronger in the rural than urban areas. Factors like illiteracy, poverty, and ignorance combine to produce such an ugly situation of women marginalization.

The result of two-way ANOVA used to test the variance of the Dominion Centre men and women on their views on women empowerment indicated a significant difference: $F(3,19)=2.09$; $P<.05$. It means that the masculine and feminine views on women empowerment in the church are strongly stratified and not unified. The earlier percentile difference of 38.5 percent (female) and 52.5 percent (male) confirms this difference of opinion, which isn't abnormal because the impact of the Gospel cannot be at the same degree for all the men and women in the church.

From the Appreciative Inquiry interview, almost all the male respondents indicated that the love and care in the church was a significant mark of the church. They desired that such love would continue to grow among the members. Most of the males, 80 percent, agreed that the celebration of the Annual Charismatic Women League (CWL) program was always a turning point in the life of the church. They appreciated all the sacrifices of the women during this one-week annual event. This form of appreciation should reflect in other aspects of the women's life, and, more importantly, the male dominated leadership should ensure that their efforts to appreciate the women are perceived to be so.

Analysis of Evaluation of Intervention Program (A.I.)
and Women Empowerment Seminar

I tested the effectiveness of the seminar on women's empowerment with a four-item questionnaire that revealed the level of positive impact of the seminar as well as the Appreciative Inquiry interview on the attitudes of the participants on women empowerment. It was obtained from the evaluation of the participants on the subject matter as well as the positive impact of the seminar on women empowerment. The questionnaire is shown in appendix E. Consequently, after administering the intervention (the 4-D Cycle of A.I), this questionnaire was given to the participants.

The result of the four items on the evaluation questionnaire of the intervention and women empowerment seminar (given to forty participants of the study, (ten for each gender in the two churches), revealed the following trend of thoughts and observations. This evaluation was carried out in January 2016. The seminar was held in November 2015. First, both males and females agreed that women empowerment in the Charismatic Renewal Ministries was a reality and has experienced significant improvement after the women empowerment seminar was held. This result revealed a positive impact of the intervention program and women empowerment seminar on the participants based on their scores before and after the intervention and seminar. For Holy Ghost Church women, it was 41.5 percent before and 60 percent after and for the men, 62.5 percent before 70 percent after. For Dominion Center female participants the result was 38.5 percent before and 20 percent (good) and 50 percent (fair) after, and for the males it was 32.8 percent and 60 percent after. This result of the evaluation shows positive significant improvement in the views of males and females in both Charismatic Churches in Lagos State, Nigeria. It shows that the intervention program was relevant, useful and effective. In my own opinion, this intervention program may be useful in other centers of Charismatic Renewal Ministries and churches.

With regard to the issue of the impact of their participation in the seminar, 90 percent of both male and female in the Holy Ghost Church affirmed that it was significant. For Dominion Church the results were 60 percent for males and 100 percent for females. The two churches noted that the impact was significantly positive. They further expressed their verbal desire for the church to continue the program on women empowerment.

With regard to the question of the benefits of the women empowerment program, in the Holy Ghost Church 90 percent of both genders opined that it was useful, while in the Dominion centre the results were 60 percent for females and 70 percent for males. I think that the uniqueness and novelty of the women empowerment program also boosted the status of the program.

Surprisingly, in both churches, more males expressed their desire for the women empowerment seminar to continue than females (100 percent versus 80 percent respectively). The crucial issue is that both genders desired that the women empowerment seminar program continue.

The remaining 20 percent of the women expressed the opinion that the women empowerment program should be carried out sometimes as against often and always. Remarkably, the view of holding women empowerment program often and not always is still positive. The wisdom in this expressed opinion is to accommodate other church programs.

The opinion of the Holy Ghost Church males and females tended to be more in agreement with each other than those of their colleagues in Dominion Centre. The likely reason is that the participants in the former church are better placed socioeconomically.

In conclusion I think that both the intervention program and the seminar on women empowerment had positive significant impact on both male and female participants. It was a worthwhile exercise that needs to be replicated in other churches and organizations.

Recommendations

Church leaders in the Charismatic Renewal Ministries have a great opportunity to learn from women the challenges marginalizing Christian women create among the latter as well as how to provide solutions. Church leaders in the Charismatic Renewal Ministries, Lagos State and indeed worldwide can use the following strategies to empower women, which will as well be of great benefit to the entire body of Christ.

Supportive Male Attitude

The women empowerment program would benefit immensely from every form of support from men. Like someone rightly said that when creating Eve, God didn't take from Adam's legs; as a proof that He doesn't want Adam to oppress Eve (woman); neither did God take part of Adam's head as a proof that Eve (woman) should oppress Adam (man). The idea of using Adam's rib to create Eve is a demonstration of divine approval for equality and partnership of the genders.

The traditional attitude of most African men towards women empowerment is at best hypocritical. Most African men agree that women are the weaker vessels but we refuse to accept that (men) are weak. The judgment is that if women are weaker, then men are stronger. Yet the comparative truth is that, if women are weaker, men are weak. The weak and weaker need to cooperate and complement each other instead of competing and fighting against themselves.

Another irony is that the African males in spite of understanding that women are the weaker vessels, and therefore should be provided and protected, go on to belabor the latter. These women are home makers, child bearers, cooks, gardeners, cleaners, and sometimes breadwinners of the home. Can weaker vessels perform all these functions and still remain faithful lovers, and dutiful wives?

I believe the right attitude is to support the women in all their numerous tasks. Men need to show greater and regular appreciation towards women. The result will be healthy relationships and greater levels of success in every life endeavour in society.

In other words, both genders can attain their best results when they support each other. Women empowerment in the church and society will experience exponential progress when the males change their negative attitudes towards females and move from pillars of female marginalization to vanguards of women empowerment. This partnership underscores the principle of interdependence.[1] The theory enunciates that human beings undergo three stages of life viz. dependence, independence, and interdependence. Every mortal all begins childhood with total dependence on others and grow into the period of striving to be independent and finally discover the power of interdependence in adulthood.

I think that this theory of interdependence can be understood beyond physical development and instead be viewed as the degree of mental and emotional (psychological) development. Consequently, some physical adults are fixated or even suffer retrogression in their level of psychological development. Mental and emotional development therefore is a major task for males who would be instrumental in this program of women empowerment. Male engagement in such program that will enable them to support women empowerment will redound to the benefit of the church and society.

Early and continuous enlightenment for men

My observation is that ignorance is a major cause of human tragedy. On the contrary, knowledge is power. Furthermore, I think that a significant cause of male chauvinism and the consequent effort of women marginalization is ignorance. This lack of knowledge of women by men affects various spheres of the former's life, such as divine purpose for creating women, their potential, pains, strengths and weaknesses.

One effective way to achieve quality enlightenment is to begin at the family level. Normally the home is the first school we attend, while parents are our first teachers. The enlightenment and educational program on gender equality and empowerment should begin there. Parents should avoid engaging in any form of gender marginalization and enslavement. Next, the education of gender and, particularly, women empowerment should continue in the school and church.

---

[1] Stephen R. Covey, *The 7 Habits of Highly Effective People* (New York: Simon & Schuster, 1999).

Consequently, providing educational and enlightenment programs for men and women will facilitate the development of positive attitude towards women as well as enhance masculine efforts towards women empowerment. These educational and enlightenment programs should proceed in two ways – at the early stage of masculine development (male children)as well as deliberate efforts to maintain such program at the different levels of masculine development.

Attitudinal change is crucial for achievement and success in every aspect of life. Attitudes are more important than several other issues of life.[2] One educational and enlightenment material that will enhance the masculine appreciation of women empowerment is the seminar used in this study. Both male and female participants showed their appreciation of the material.

Legislation on Women Empowerment

An African proverb says that livestock owed by everybody belongs to nobody. The relevance of this axiom is in connection with women empowerment. Some people question the need to seek legislation for women empowerment and not for men.

The reasons are obvious. First, in most societies and churches, the leadership is dominated by men. Again this male dominance of leadership has been prevalent for a long period to the level where it has become normative and systemic. Worse still, the victims of male domination of leadership and policy making has negatively impacted women so immensely that the latter have become reluctant to lead.

Consequently, I believe all these negative attitudes towards women create the need for the legislation of women empowerment programs. Both society and church, or any other organization where women play active roles, should make deliberate plans to give women appropriate and proportional portions of power, opportunities, and status. I believe all these recommendations on women empowerment should be backed by law and followed up by consistent implementation. For instance, the

---

[2] Zig Ziglar, *Over the Top* (Nashville, TN: Thomas Nelson, 1997).

Nigerian government has only implemented 5 percent of affirmation policy on promoting the idea of women in government.[3]

Unfortunately the Nigerian Senate (highest legislative body) rejected a bill on equality of the genders March 2016. The gender equality bill was presented by Mrs. Abiodun Olujimi, representing Ekiti South, (South West, Nigeria) in the Nigeria Senate. It was entitled, "Gender Party and Prohibition of Violence Against Women"[4] Two major factors that truncated this gender empowerment bill were religious bigotry and male chauvinism.

This Nigerian male negative attitude towards female empowerment reminded me that mortals are truly resistant to change. I think that mortals are deeply trapped in the mire of self-preservation and egotism. Imagine the new lease of life and breakthrough the Nigerian nation would have experienced if the bill of equality of gender was successfully passed into law. I believe that the impact would have been incredibly positive.

The church and particularly Charismatic Renewal Ministries, Lagos State can promote women empowerment by legislating that a significant percentage of women must be represented in every cadre of spiritual leadership. The other crucial aspect of legislation is implementation of the policy. It is as important as the signing into law a policy on favourable women empowerment.

Favourable Policy on Career Empowerment

Any covert or overt policy that promotes the idea that women are only good at home front tasks isn't only offensive but oppressive towards women. Women can participate effectively in both blue and white collar jobs. Contemporarily, there is hardly any noble profession that women

---

[3] Kolade Larewaju, "Nigeria Has Implemented Five Percent (5%) of Affirmative Action on Women,", Feminista News, http://www.vanguardngr.com/2015/07/nigeria-has-implemented-only-five-percent-of-affirmative-action-on-women-okunuga/ (accessed August 2015).

[4] Abiodun Olujimi, "Gender Parity and Prohibition of Violence Against Women" Quoted in Timothy Oshi, "Nigerian Senate Rejects Bill Seeking Gender Equally in Marriage," *Premium Times*, March 15, 2016, accessed May 10, 2016, http://Senate –rejects bill-seeking-gender-equ.

aren't involved in: from educational to electronics, medical to pharmaceutical, aviation to agriculture, ministerial to marketing.

More remarkably, some of these women are excelling in these hitherto male dominated careers. With adequate encouragement from men, these women can achieve greater heights.

Perhaps the most appropriate beginning point to prepare women for career empowerment is providing them with quality education. Education is the needed leverage that enhances the value of labour.

Unfortunately, in traditional African society, the culture was to marry girls immediately after reaching puberty. Even after the coming of Western education through the missionaries, most African homes permitted the males to engage in Western education but resisted the idea of allowing females to benefit from it. The picture of many African homes was that of an educated husband and half-illiterate wife.

Consequently, the women were constrained to be relevant only in the home front. This scenario is changing to favour the liberation of women from illiteracy. It is therefore necessary to pursue the policy of educational empowerment of women which will result to a state of favourable career empowerment.

Economic Empowerment

The idea that money answers to all things (Eccl. 10:19) may be an extreme, one but it is nonetheless significant. Just as the love of money is the root of all evil (2 Tim. 6:10), the lack of money is at foundation of most evils. A situation whereby the predominant male leadership in the society and church deny women the opportunity to create and own wealth is narcissistic and inhuman.

In some very pitiable situations, there are wives who are subjected to a complete begging policy. In such an abnormal situation, the woman depends entirely on the husband's earning for all her monetary needs, while at the same time, the man is unhappy that the wife isn't earning any income.

Many men cannot resist the temptation of using monetary power to control the lives of their wives. Consequently, the women may be reduced to the status of a beggar or liability in the home and church. In other to avoid the temptation of destroying the personality of the woman through male manipulation of monetary power, the woman needs to be economically empowered.

Some of the avenues for empowering women economically include exposure to appropriate education, career training, apprenticeship training, mentoring and provision of capital for small and medium sized businesses. It is remarkable to note that some of the women who attended to Jesus' material needs did so from their personal resources (Luke 8:1-3). They were economically empowered women.

Therefore, I note that God wants women to be economically independent. He created them with potential, abilities, and skills, which if developed and deployed will bring forth various degrees of economic harvest.

Encourage Education of Women

The traditional African position that educating a male child is more profitable to the family and, by extension, the larger society than the female should be totally jettisoned. The church should show genuine and continuous interest as well as deliberately invest in the formal education of women. Churches should champion the plan of building schools and ensure that every female child from the church gets quality education. From such a wonderful example the church can then champion the course of female education in the larger society.

I find it unimaginable to think of a world without Helen Keller, Indira Ghandi, Margaret Thatcher, and many other women who distinguished (still distinguish) themselves in different spheres of life. The foundation of this feminine distinction is quality education. No stage should be neglected; from nursery to primary, to secondary, and finally tertiary levels. The church should first show example by encouraging and enforcing the education of her female children as well as champion the same in the society. Christian leaders should become the vanguards of female education. Encouraging female education will surely impact positively on the health and progress of the family and other human institutions such as business, politics, and governance.

The ugly cases of female children used for street trading can be reversed. Several other cases of child labour, girls and women reduced to sex slaves and beasts of burden can be upturned by a conscientious plan by church leaders in every African community and city. At some point in the pursuit of the vision of education for all females, the introduction of scholarship schemes would be inevitable. The introduction of scholarship is a possible vision as far as the male dominated leadership of the church sees the need to educate the female child. Education is the passport to success in modern world and individuals need to pay any price to empower others to obtain the qualitative version. Most females who obtain education is obviously on the right path to empowerment and success. I hope it becomes my passion and vision to assist many females to acquire qualitative education.

Encourage Female Giftedness

I believe that the true value of feminine positive impact in any community or city is determined by the population of undeveloped gifts and talents. Considered in this light, in most African churches and society, the result is regrettably wasteful. The reason is because there exist a huge percentage of untapped and unexplored feminine resources in the church and society.

In the contemporary world, women are breaking barriers as well as creating new records as they enter careers and professions that were in the past exclusively reserved for men. From engineering and technology, medical and pharmaceutical, entertainment and economic, to neuroscience and space science, there is hardly any sphere of human endeavour that women have not ventured into as well as conquered, which is commendable and should be sustained.

As I noted earlier, acquiring qualitative education is the solid foundation for attaining success in the world today. Consequently to consolidate the gains of the success of education, care should be taken to ensure that the girls are encouraged to discover and develop their God-given, talents, and gifts. The girls should be encouraged to acquire both general and special education.

No doubt, the training of professional manpower is costly in terms of financial and time resources. Yet, what is good for the goose (male) should be considered to be good for the gander (female). The discrimination against females in this area of investment to identify and develop their skills should be totally eradicated. There exists no empirical evidence that male professionals in any given field of human endeavour are superior to their female counterparts.

The point is made that given equal opportunities; female professionals may achieve significantly similar positive results as their male counterparts. The challenge is that of giving or providing equal opportunity to females to discover, develop, and deploy their gifts and talents.

Conclusion

The focus of this chapter was to present and analyze the data of the findings of males and females in two churches of Charismatic Renewal Ministries, Lagos State. Thereafter, recommendations were given based on the analysis of the findings. The questionnaires provided closed responses, while the interviews provided detailed explanation of the research focus. The participants responses complemented each other.

The analysis of the questionnaire was carried out by the use of Social Science Statistical Package (SSSP) and the result was further strengthened by the use 2-way Analysis of Variance (ANOVA). Four groups were identified for the study as male and female church leaders from Charismatic Renewal Ministries, Dominion Center, Egbe and the same for Holy Ghost Church Surulere, Lagos. The former church center is a suburban area, while the latter is an urban area. In the issues of response to appreciation of women and cultural practices there were similarities. However in terms of how both genders responded to women empowerment, as well as women perception of male dominated leadership, there were differences in opinion. Finally, recommendations were proffered. It was an interesting and challenging exercise. The next chapter is a summary and conclusion of the research work.

CHAPTER 7

SUMMARY AND CONCLUSION

Introduction

This last chapter takes a retrospective view and attempts to present the summary of research conclusions, recommendations, and possible areas of future research. In the previous chapters the focus was presentation of the problem of study, hypothesis, and review of literature from both biblical theology and secular viewpoint. Also the methodology of the research was explained and finally recommendations were proffered.

Summary

This study used the strategy of Appreciative Inquiry to empower Charismatic Renewal Ministries women in Lagos State, Nigeria. The study also highlighted the role of men, culture, and ignorance of Scripture in marginalizing women.

The need was that women should be accorded more positions of leadership in the church. Furthermore, the strategies for achieving this greater appreciation of women in the Charismatic Renewal Ministries were proffered.

There was a review of literature on the strategic plans of empowering Charismatic women. The historical background as well as the current situation on the matters of concern to Charismatic women was highlighted. Other crucial matters relating to the research topic that were highlighted were marginalization of women in the church and women empowerment in the Charismatic Renewal Ministries. Also, the theological background of women empowerment was enunciated.

The design of choice for the study was descriptive survey, which specially enabled the use of questionnaire and structured interview. The questionnaire had two different formats for males and females. However the interview schedule was the same for both genders. Of the one eighty questionnaires distributed for the study, eighty were returned, representing a total of 100 percent, which was significant enough for the proof of validity and reliability. In the case of the interviews, there were twenty of them scheduled and held. The crucial issues of the study such as validity, reliability, and objectivity were handled by pretesting the instruments before administering them to the participants. Themes emerged based on the congruency of items of the instruments. Data was collected, collated, summarized, and interpreted. The SPSS program for presentation and analysis was used. This design was considered adequate in accordance with the aim of the study to reveal the views and belief of the Charismatic leadership on women empowerment as well as help them to improve on how to empower women.

The result of the research indicated that both males and females differed in their views and appreciation of women empowerment. Fundamentally, men opined that the level of women empowerment in the church was favourably significant on various issues such as education, career, family life, and even in spiritual matters. But the women, while acknowledging that the church leadership practices some level of women empowerment, desired that there should be greater and more concrete programs geared towards improving the degree of women empowerment. Furthermore, the study revealed that because of the crucial position men occupy as leaders in the church, which necessarily has positioned them to contribute to the marginalization of women, the former should join hands with women to pursue the noble task of improving the level of women empowerment in the church. Men should learn to be complementary instead of competitors' or worse still aggressors against women.

Furthermore, the findings of the study revealed that women tend to be reluctant to assume leadership positions in the church. However the underlying cause of this problem was attributed to the two main reasons. First was the issue of the prevalence of African culture that tends to marginalize and oppress women. Again the unconscious transfer of this oppressive policy against women into the church for a long period of time has negatively impacted both men and women to accept women marginalization as being normal. I recommend that men and women need to be educated and enlightened on the issue of women empowerment.

Consequently, I recommend that the exposure of both genders to matters on women empowerment should begin early in life and be carried out consistently. Women are not less endowed than men. For example, the Charismatic Renewal Ministries in the past have had women leaders in all the levels of leadership – local, zonal, state, regional, and national. The first State Representative of Gongola in the early 1980s (now Adamawa) Mrs. Felicia Agbahia, is a woman. Dr. Adeola Ilechukwu isn't just the wife of the General Overseer of Charismatic Renewal Ministries Incorporated, she is a gifted prophetess, erudite teacher, and astute academician. These two church women leaders and others performed and continue to perform excellently in their roles. It then shows that if more women are allowed or encouraged to lead, they will likely prove their mettle. The desired line of action is for the church leadership to encourage a greater degree of women empowerment in every sphere of the church life and particularly in the area of leadership in the church. In the same light there are other women who occupy sensitive positions in the leadership of Charismatic Renewal Ministries. I hope the light of the Gospel continues to shine more along the line of greater women empowerment.

Conclusions

This section of conclusion will try to capture the summary of the entire project. Based on the research sub-questions in chapter 1, and derived on the results and findings outlined in chapter 6, the following conclusions are made.

Peculiar Challenges Facing Women in Obtaining Empowerment

The results of the study revealed that women face some obstacles in obtaining greater empowerment in the Charismatic Renewal Ministries. Some of the factors implicated as posing peculiar obstacles to women empowerment in the church are lack of personal confidence, inferiority complex, self-rejection, jealousy and envy among women, pettiness, and extreme emotionalism. Other peculiar challenges include cultural biases against women and the pursuit of female liberation agenda that men perceive to be confrontational instead of being ameliorative. Some of these peculiar obstacles to women empowerment has been confirmed and collaborated by other researchers like Hove[1] and Ettu.[2]

Provision of Empowerment for Christian Women

The study confirmed that there exists some degree of women empowerment in the Charismatic Renewal Ministries, Lagos State Nigeria, but that there exists a greater opportunity for improvement. The research revealed that unintentionally there exists a gap between the church leadership official position on women empowerment and the real practice. This gap can be filled by the cooperation of the male leaders and the women. The solution can never be achieved by negative attitudes such as denial of reality and negligence on behalf of the church leadership nor stubbornness and lack of confidence on the side of the women.

In the early years of the Charismatic Renewal Ministries, when the members were virtually all youths on campus, the level of women empowerment was unquestionably high. The issue of raising new homes and parenting must have affected the level of women empowerment in the church. This research provides a great opportunity to bring the needed restoration.

Strategies to Be Used to Address These Challenges

I think that one of the greatest obstacles to human development is ignorance. For instance, in the issue of relationship between men and women, ignorance fans the embers of negative attitudes such as fear, jealousy, hatred, and, ultimately, oppression. However, the truth is that men and women are complements and not competitors. They are friends

---

[1] Hove, 20.

[2] Ettu, 84.

and not fiends. The main reason that both males and females need to have a harmonious relationship is because both genders have the same Source. God created them male and female (Gen. 1:26, 27).

Consequently, men and women can cooperate to solve the problem of lack of women appreciation and empowerment. First, men should take the lead in the empowerment program of women in the church, just as they contributed to the marginalization. Both genders should collaborate to eliminate retrogressive cultural biases that hinder women empowerment, while the women should conscientiously take the task of receiving education to deal with internal feminine problems such as inferiority complex and fear.

Recommendations for Women to improve the Degree of Women Empowerment

1. Charismatic women should use every opportunity to obtain quality education in relevant areas. The improvement in education will improve their positions in leadership both in the church and society.
2. Charismatic women should specifically get involved in theological education in order to reposition themselves for spiritual or ecclesiastical leadership.
3. Charismatic women should deliberately be involved in a mentoring relationship, which would provide a practical platform for the demonstration of self-confidence.
4. Synergy is one of the best principles of success. Consequently, Charismatic women would benefit from a deliberate policy of cooperation and collaboration with men. One practical way to achieve synergy between the two genders is to encourage regular exchange of ideas during joint organized seminars, teachings, and programs.
5. Charismatic women can further improve their self-confidence by working in unity among themselves and by encouraging others to improve their socio-economy.
6. An axiom says that success has many friends, while failure has many enemies. Consequently, charismatic women can improve their opportunities of empowerment through upholding a deliberate policy of excellent lifestyle.

Recommendation to the Church Leadership

1. Expand the curriculum of the marriage committee (MC) to include enlightenment of couples during courtship in the issue of women empowerment.
2. Develop a policy of appreciating the role of women in every sphere of church life.
3. Include topics on women empowerment in the church Sunday school manual. The seminar paper used in this study can be adopted and adapted for such an event.
4. Encourage girls' education in every primary and secondary school that belongs to the church. One particular way of achieving the goal of encouraging girl's education is by offering yearly scholarship.
5. Discover and determine some particular aspects of church leadership that are based on giftings, abilities, and skills. On some occasions, women are the best suitable candidates and should be deliberately deployed to occupy such positions.
6. Provide equal opportunities for females and males to occupy every church leadership position.
7. Establish a policy of equal honour and remuneration for female and male ministers or leaders.
8. Regularly dialogue with women at various stages of the church life to find out how to improve on the issue of women empowerment.

Areas of Future Research

For the purpose of improvement in research work in related issues of women and men, there is need to take the following steps.

1. Carry out a family members assessment on women empowerment. The views of children, youths, single adults, and parents may disagree or agree.
2. Compare and contrast the subject of women empowerment in the Charismatic Renewal Ministries in different countries and continents.
3. Consider how to raise a new generation of charismatic men who are totally liberated from negative African cultural influence that is against women empowerment.

Action Plan for Women Empowerment in Charismatic Renewal Ministries:
A Fourfold Personal Transformational Model

Considered from every angle, the subject of empowerment is a positive one. It has to do with improvement of life, provision of resources, and enablement, which, when realized, benefits all the parties involved. For instance, education of the female child can result into amazing benefits for the individual, family, church, and society.

Consequently I propose a four-stage model for empowering women in the Charismatic Renewal Ministries. This women empowerment model can be adopted and adapted by any other churches or societies seriously interested in the transformation of women. The four stages of women empowerment are Attraction, Attention, Allocation, and Approval. The nucleus of all of these 4 stages is Divine Affection (Love, Agape).

Attraction Stage

This first stage of women empowerment in the church focuses on attracting women both inside and outside the church to the love of God (Divine Affection). Ironically some members of the church (both male and female) are far-distanced from Divine Affection. The attitude of distancing oneself from God is why Isaiah speaks of "comforting those who mourn in Zion" (61:1-3). The focus is helping people (women in particular) to experience salvation and the approach are proclamation and demonstration of the Good News. Those who respond positively to the attractive strategies receive divine love, which is the foundation of genuine and enduring empowerment.

Also crisis in faith issues such as double mindedness/unbelief (James 1:5-7) discouragement, drawing back, or outright backsliding exist in the church. Christians who are involved in such circumstances, which tend to harm or deflate their faith in God, need to be reassured of God's faithfulness and care in their present circumstances.

Consequently as the light of the world and salt of the earth, the church leadership can mobilize the church to regain the lost sheep inside (in Zion) as well as reclaim others outside. The target of restoration of the lost insiders and outsiders will involve the following strategies.

Proclamation of the Gospel

The church leadership should ensure that the real Gospel is preached regularly. Often some witnesses and preachers of the Gospel fail to present the Goodnews. Also I think that some believers concentrate on presenting church or creed, denomination or doctrine. In like manner, I think that others focus on magnifying the devil, his works or sin or mankind's weaknesses. All negative approaches work against the prosperity of the Gospel. The church leadership should present the Good News that Jesus is the solution to the human problems of sin, selfishness, and human weaknesses as well as all satanic oppressions. Jesus came to seek and save the lost and not to condemn them. He calls all to come to Him and be saved. Only those who reject the call will be damned (John 3:16-21, Matt. 11:28-31).

Demonstration of Christ-like Character

Equally, it is very important that the lives of believers reflect what we proclaim. A common axiom says that actions speaks louder than words. Walking the talk authenticates the message of Christ. It is still the duty of the church leadership to ensure that the lives of the members reflect the character of the Master. Ensuring that members reflect the life of Christ has to do with the fruit of the Spirit (Gal. 5:22-26).

In practice, the demonstration of Christ-like character will involve the church engaging in activities like social action, which will alleviate the problems of people in the church and society. Examples of such social actions are provision of welfare for the needy, free medical services, and economic empowerment programs. Jesus cared for the whole personality of humanity. The church should follow the Master's example.

Demonstration of Christ-like Power

For many others, the secret of attracting them to Christ lies in the demonstration of divine power such as casting out of demons, healing the sick, accessing divine revelation, and obtaining divine intervention. Particularly for women, this strategy is very effective in attracting them to Christ.

However, this order will suffice for the lost outsiders, but for those who mourn in Zion (lost insiders), the process will begin with the three demonstration strategies. The obvious reason for the change of order of presentation is due to the fact that the lost insiders are searching for demonstration and not necessarily the proclamation of the Gospel.

Attention Stage

In the previous stage of attraction, success is measured by the degree of affirmation to the attractive strategies of the church. It is like delivering a baby safely, which is the new birth. In this second stage, the focus is discovery of gifting and abilities, and it is carried out by teaching. It can be likened to grooming. The strategies at this stage are teaching and exemplary leadership, while the right responses are desire to learn as well as being teachable.

As a member of the Body of Christ as well as a local assembly, the woman would be assigned to a small Bible study class where she would be discipled. The peculiarity of this grooming or discipling stage is to discover the entrepreneurial ability and gifting of the woman. By providing quality attention to the new member of the church, her empowerment potentials will be discovered.

At this attention stage, the seminar on Women Empowerment should be introduced. Contrary to traditional African belief system, the woman is an asset and not a liability; she is to be seen and heard and not to be regarded as an ornament. Adopting an entire repertoire of positive attitude towards women in the church will enhance the discovery and development of their potentials.

Allocation Stage

The focus of the allocation stage of women empowerment is to achieve maximum development of women's potentials. It will produce harmony between the women and their giftings and abilities. The strategies are intensive training, mentoring, assignment of individual, and group activities. The expected positive response at this stage is acquisition of skill.

After the discovery of the skills and abilities of the woman, efforts should be geared towards training her to develop her potentials and possibilities. The second part of the seminar on Women Empowerment will be useful at this stage. In other words, the woman is allocated to her area of specialization from the outset of the class. Engaging the woman in mentoring, supervision, and group projects will enhance the attainment of the goal of harmony at this stage of empowerment.

Approval Stage

This final stage of women empowerment focuses on achieving a healthy integration of the character (virtue) and ability of the woman. It is focused on attainment of excellence in character and abilities. It is the integration of integrity and intelligence. The church leadership ensures that the woman responds positively to the attractive stage and receives appropriate attention and allocation. When all these three stages have been completed by the woman, the church leadership now gives approval of attainment of personal transformation that is manifest in empowerment.

Approval stage is like graduation stage or the release of the eaglet after undergoing strenuous training of the mother eagle. This transformational model of women empowerment in the Charismatic Renewal Ministries, Lagos State is represented in table 9.

Table 9. Diagram of Four Stage Transformational Model of Women Empowerment

S/N	Stages	Responses		Focus	Nucleus	Strategy
		Positive	Negative			
1	Attraction	Reception	Rejection	Personal Salvation	Divine Affection	Proclamation of Good News. Demonstration of God News.
2	Attention	Learning	Fixation	Discovery of Gifting	Divine Affection	Teaching Exemplary leadership
3	Allocation	Acquisation of skills	Personal Distress	Development of Gifting (Harmony)	Divine Affection	Training Mentoring Group Activities Individual assignment
4	Approval	Fulfilment Joy	Sorrow/Disappointment	Integration of character and abilities to achieve excellence.	Divine Affection	Examination Practical tests/sessions projects.

From table 9, Divine Love (Agape) is at the centre (nucleus) of transformation and empowerment. In order words, neither personal transformation nor empowerment can take place outside God's love. It is personal and positive response to God's love (Agape) that ushers in empowerment. Each of the four stages of empowerment and transformation focuses on a progressive attainment step, while each stage employs the use of some particular strategies to achieve the required goal. Furthermore, at every stage, there exist positive and negative responses to the strategies used to demonstrate Divine Love. Positive response leads to growth and progress, while negative responses lead to stagnation and retrogression. When applied properly, this model of women empowerment will produce significant results. It can be adapted and adopted by the entire church.

Personal Implementation of Fourfold Personal Transformational Model

There are two strategies of implementing this fourfold personal transformational model for women. The first is by organizing two annual empowerment seminars for women (March and September) in churches with the collaboration of church leaders.

These women empowerment seminars would focus on the different aspects of a woman's life based on the principles of divine affection and employing the fourfold transformational model of Attraction, Attention, Allocation, and Approval. A fundamental condition for organizing this twice annual women empowerment seminar is to secure the assurance that the male leaders of the church or organization will participate actively in the seminars. The issue of significant male participation in the women empowerment program is to enhance the result because collaboration between the two genders facilitates the goal of empowerment.

The second and major practical strategy to implement this fourfold personal transformational model of women empowerment is to organize an Annual Couples Get-Together (First Saturday of every December), where the principles of Attraction, Attention, Allocation, and Approval will be taught. Furthermore, the occasion will serve as a relaxation opportunity for couples to renew their affection for God and each other. In contemporary world, many couples are driven by the tyranny of lack of time and space for each other. These annual Couples Get-Togethers will provide both opportunity and time for couples to invest in each other's life as well as grow in intimacy, which will enrich the lives of many marriages. Consequently, an enriched and healthy marriage is a sure avenue for women empowerment.

Summary and Conclusion

The focus of this dissertation was using Appreciative Inquiry as a strategy to empower Charismatic Renewal Ministries Women, Lagos State, Nigeria. In using Appreciative Inquiry, I recognized the already existing proofs of women empowerment in the Lagos branch of the Charismatic Renewal Ministries such as encouraging the education of women, allowing women to be involved in some level of leadership as well as encouraging them to pursue their God-given careers.

Also I considered the impact of African culture, tradition and ignorance on the marginalization and empowerment of women in the church. Furthermore, I established the biblical foundation of the study by considering some relevant core issues such as career, leadership and family life.

The use of AI seminar as an intervention strategy to improve the need for women empowerment among the leadership and membership of the Charismatic Church in Lagos State, Nigeria yielded a positive result. Both males and females leaders of the church agreed to take practical steps to pursue a policy of women empowerment. The use of the seminar document was a welcome idea in the Charismatic church, Lagos State.

To sustain and promote women empowerment in the Charismatic Church and society, I obliged to hold an annual women empowerment seminar. As challenging as it will be to hold such an annual seminar, I will do my best to keep at it.

In general, I conclude that engaging in this dissertation on women empowerment was both challenging and crucial, interesting and inspiring. I hope that it will attract significant attention from the church leadership of Charismatic Renewal Ministries and other churches. Also, it will attract the attention of leaders in other organizations so that both the church and society will experience transformation. I return all the glory to God for the completion of this dissertation. I strongly believe that God will use the findings to catalyze positive changes in Nigeria and beyond.

APPENDIX A
RELATIONSHIP BETWEEN MALES AND FEMALES IN OUR CHURCH

Section A

This first section contains **20** questions and answers ranging from 5 to 1 in terms of strongly agree to not at all. Please mark the answer which represents your understanding.

S/N	QUESTION	Strongly Agree	Averagely Agree	Weakly Agree	Not at all
1.	In our church both males and females enjoy a cordial relationship.				
2.	As a female leader I feel safe in our church.				
3.	As a female leader I enjoy my status and role.				
4.	I enjoy the support of other female leaders.				
5.	Women leaders outnumber male leaders in our church.				
6.	Women are better leaders than men.				
7.	As a female leader my supervisors listen more to me than my male colleagues.				
8.	As a female leader my subordinates cooperate more with me than my male colleagues.				
9.	Generally female leaders are preferred to males in our church.				
10.	Husbands accept and affirm their wives.				
11.	Families with female leaders enjoy more harmony than those with males.				
12.	As a female leader I enjoy equal financial income with male colleagues.				
13.	I enjoy a sense of harmony among male leaders.				

	Strongly Agree	Averagely Agree	Weakly Agree	Not at all
14. I enjoy harmony among fellow female leaders				
15. I would gladly be a member of a church led by a woman.				
16. I will vote a fellow woman into leadership position.				
17. I will gladly obey women leadership.				
18. I freely exercise my spiritual gift in the church.				
19. There is no limitation to my career development.				
20. I can freely express my opinion in our church.				

APPENDIX B
APPRECIATIVE INQUIRY QUESTIONNAIRE FOR MALE LEADERS

Dear participant,

This questionnaire isn't an examination. It is an opinion pool which respects each person's view. Also note that there is complete anonymity for your response.

PURPOSE: This questionnaire is part of the instruments being used by the researcher to gather data for his Doctor of Ministry in the above mentioned University. The study employs Appreciative Inquiry (AI) approach to discover the degree of women empowerment in the Charismatic Renewal Ministries, Lagos State.

Please answer and score these questions on this four point scale from your personal perception (view point).

BIOGRAPHICAL DATA

Leadership position

	Not at all	Scarcely	Averagely	Always
Leadership				
1. Many women in our church are appointed to lead.				
2. It is normal for women in our church to lead groups constituting of both males and females.				
3. Males in our church approve of female leadership.				
4. Male in our church are delighted with female leadership.				
Education				
5. Most women in our church are educated.				
6. Our church encourages women education.				
7. Males in our church approve of women education.				

	Not at all	Scarcely	Averagely	Always
8. Our church has a program/project centered at encouraging women education.				
Economic				
9. Most women in our church are rich.				
10. Our church encourages women to be economically independent				
11. Males in our church encourage women to be economically independent				
12. Our church leadership has a program for empowering women economically.				
Marital				
13. Every woman in our church enjoys her marriage.				
14. Out church encourages women to enjoy their marriage.				
15.Husbands in our church work diligently so that their wives can enjoy their marriage.				

	Not at all	Scarcely	Averagely	Always
16. Our church has a marriage counseling programme geared towards helping wives to enjoy their homes.				
Mental 17. Every woman in our church is mentally sound.				
18. Our church encourages the mental health of women.				
19. Men in our church facilitate the mental health/developme nt of women.				
20. Our church deliberately encourages the mental development of women.				

INTERVIEW

I am Passy Anayo Amaraegbu, a doctorate student with Bakke Graduate University (BGU), USA. A requirement for my completing the program. I am conducting a research entitled, "Appreciative Inquiry As a potent strategy for empowering the Women of Charismatic Renewal Ministries, Lagos State, Nigeria" my focus is the Charismatic Church in Lagos State.

I joined the ministry in Lagos State in 1986, pastured, Dominion Centre Egbe from 1994-2001, served as the State Overseer from 2002-2014 and is now the Overseer of Lagos State One, after the last year structural adjustment. As one selected to participate in this study, your sincere contribution will enhance the quality of the study. Equally it will contribute to the health and growth of the church and society.

Please answer all the questions as honestly as possible

Venue of interviews: _____

Date: _____

Questions 1 to 15
1. Describe a time when you felt that the group (Charismatic Renewal Ministries, at the Local and State levels) performed really well.

    _____

    _____

2. Identify at least two circumstances of such occasion.

    _____

    _____

3. Describe a time when you were proud to be a member of the group/ministry (Provide at least 2 instances)

_____

_____

4. What were the circumstances that touched your heart during that period.

_____

_____

5. Describe (at least two occasions) when male and female leaders in your ministry complemented (worked together) with each other to achieve success.

_____

_____

6. Describe the type of positive feelings you experienced as well as the impact such positive synergy had on you.

_____

_____

7. What positive impact has the practice of new testament culture made on the African cultural way of valuing women in your church?

_____

_____

8. Describe the degree of satisfaction this practice of new testament scriptural culture has made in women of your church.

_____

9. What were you proud of in the leadership of your church (at least 3)

_____

_____

10. What other things are you proud of in your church?

_____

_____

11. What do you value most about being a member of this church?

_____

_____

12. Why do you value these (them)?

_____

_____

13. What are the three best wishes/desires you have for your church?

_____

_____

14. What practical ways do you think these excellent desires can be accomplished?

_____

_____

APPENDIX D.
SEMINAR ON WOMEN EMPOWERMENT
Part I (used during the Dream Stage of Appreciative Inquiry)
Reference Scripture: Gen. 1:26-28

1.0 **Introduction** – God's wisdom is infinite. Ignorance is grievously costly. For instance ignorance is one of the major reasons for the unnecessary war between males and females on the issues of superiority, roles and responsibilities.

From our reference scripture, we learn that God created male and female as two distinct human beings (v. 27). Neither is a photocopy nor shadow of the other.

Therefore why are we raising the issue of women empowerment? It is because there are proofs of marginalization. This study shall cover the following issues – meaning of Women marginalization and empowerment, examples, obstacles as well as practical ways of empowering women.

2.0 **MEANING**

2.1 **Marginalization**
   a. To make somebody feel unimportant
   b. A position of powerlessness

Therefore women marginalization involves all efforts geared towards rendering women powerless or helplessness. It is oppressive relationship against women.

2.2 **Examples of Women Marginalization**
   a. Polygamy
   b. Denial of education or even work opportunity.
   c. Negligence in health care delivery based on gender consideration.

2.3 **Empowerment**
   a. Providing someone authority or power to act.
   b. Give more control over their own lives or situation they are in.
   c. Providing resources or leverage for achievement.

d. Offering opportunities to someone for the purpose of achieving fulfillment.

Therefore empowerment involves every positive effort to help or assist somebody to attain a goal or achieve result.

2.4 Examples of Women Empowerment
   a. Raising educational fund for women.
   b. Providing quality health care for women.
   c. According women equal opportunity in government with men.

3.0 Significance Of Women Empowerment
   a. Empowering multitudes of helpless children
   b. Assisting human beings at a very critical period of life.
   c. Raising an informidable army of next generation leaders.
   d. Multiplication of Human Resources – women reproduce what you invest in their lives.

4.0 Obstacles to Women Empowerment
In our peculiar environment of Lagos, Nigeria the hinderances to women empowerment include;
   a. **Cultural Biases**
   i. The negative impact of African culture on Women empowerment such as that women are second class citizens, are predominantly childish or even foolish.
   ii. The erroneous idea that women don't need Western education. The place of the women is in the home.
   iii. Regarding wives as part of their husbands' wealth or property.

   b. **Inferiority Complex among Women**
   i. Strong feelings of poor self worth.
   ii. Desiring to be masculine is a psychological distress which afflicts many females in a male dominated society.
   iii. Disrespect, disregard and constant disagreement among women.

c. Systemic Phenomenon

Marginalization of women does not have a legal backing in Nigeria but it is institutionalized in all our systems. Most Nigerians are conscious of the superiority of males over females. This indoctrination begins from the family system and spreads to the educational, career and other areas.

d. Male Chauvaunism

The two prevailing factors that hinder women empowerment here are, the dominance of male leadership in the Nigerian society as well as their favouritism against women equal representation and emancipation.

e. High Level of illiteracy

Knowledge is poor just as ignorance is powerlessness. Knowledge liberates while ignorance limits. Consequently the predominance of illiteraly hinders every effort to empower women.

Part 2 (used during the Design Stage of Appreciative Inquiry).
5.0 **Practical Ways To Implement Women Empowerment**
This include
a. **Marriage and Family Life** *(Eph. 5:18-33, 6:1-10)*
i. Mutual respect between couples
ii. Recognition of distinct roles
iii. Practice of sacrificial love in the home.
iv. Stewardship of ability and gifts
v. Servant leadership modeled by the husband.

b. **Community Life**
i. Recognition of abilities of the genders.
ii. Division of labour.
iii. Protection of the weak and needy.

c. **Economic** *(Prov. 12:11, 24, 27)*
i. Equal opportunity for male and female genders in the labour market.
ii. No gender discrimination in terms of salaries, income and other renumerations.
iii. Providing economic leverage for marginalized women in special periods such as pregnancy, sickness, child upbringing, etc.

d. **Education**
i. Conducting enlightenment campaigns and seminars for females to motivate them to go to school.
ii. Providing equal opportunity for both genders to obtain quality education.
iii. Establishing scholarship schemes for disadvantaged females.

e. **Career** *(Matt. 25:13-e. Career (Matt. 25:13-33)*
i. Providing enabling environment for the women to make appropriate career choice.
ii. Eliminating favouritism, male chauvinism, discriminatory attitudes and all forms of marginalization tendencies against the female folk in the marketplace.
iv. According women equal opportunity with the male in the Armed forces.

f. **Politics/Governance**
i. Giving women equal opportunity as their male folk to vote and to be voted for.
ii. Giving women equal opportunity in government.
iii. Eliminating marginalization of women in every sphere of governance such as political appointments, chairpersons of parastatals, committees and boards.
iv. According women political leadership in the Armed Forces.

g. **Psychological (Mental/Emotional)**
i.   Accepting and showing affection to the girl child from the outset.
ii. Affirming and promoting femininity eat all times
iii. Encouraging both male and female genders to be accepting their statuses and distinct roles.
iv. Making provisions for the peculiar feminine expressions and emotions.

6.0 CONCLUSION

From the beginning, God made them male and female. These are two distinct complementary and not competitive human beings. The best can only come from them when both genders work and walk together as partners and neither in a master/servant own superior/inferior relationship.

As leaders of most African societies, it is our duty to reverse every instance of women marginalization. We should join hands with women to assist them excel in every life endeavour. Our society and world would be better for this. Empowering one female means empowering a multitude of people because she is connected to many human being who are at a very critical period of life – children. Empowering a woman means empowering our next generation of leaders. Let us rise up to the occasion.

APPENDIX E

EVALUATION OF PROJECT INTERVENTION/SEMINAR

Please indicate your personal opinion on the impact of participation in the Women Empowerment Seminar.

1. What is the level of Women Empowerment in the Charismatic Renewal Ministries, Lagos State?

a. Poor ☐ b. Fair ☐ c. Good ☐

d. Excellent ☐

2. How far has your participation in this Women Empowerment Seminar and program affected your views on women empowerment?

a. Not at all ☐ b. Little ☐

c. Averagely ☐ d. Significantly ☐

3. What is your personal Assessment of the benefits of this Women Empowerment program in the church?

a. Poor ☐ b. Fair ☐ c. Good ☐

d. Excellent ☐

4. Would you like the women empowerment program to continue in Charismatic Renewal Ministries?

a. Never ☐ b. Sometimes ☐ c. Often ☐

d. Always ☐

BIBLIOGRAPHY

Amaraegbu, Passy. *A Short History of the Ministry in Lagos State*. 25th Anniversary of the Ministry. [lecture], Lagos State, Nigeria.

_____. *Victory over Lust: Key to Victorious Living*. Lagos, Nigeria: Change Business Services, Ltd., 1995.

_____. "Understanding Spousal Violence." *Successful Family Magazine Beta Edition Centre for Marriage and Family Stability*, (2012).

_____. "Appreciative Inquiry of Charismatic Renewal Ministries Women." Final paper in *Overture 2: Fresno* class. Fresno, CA: Bakke Graduate University, October 2013.

Amasiatu, Ify. *Legal Challenges to Christian Life*. Port Harcourt: Nebo Christian Services, 2012.

Anglican Church of Australia. "Are Women Able to Be Priests in the Anglican Church of Australia?" http://www.anglican.org.au/home/about/students/pages/are_women_able_to_be_priests_in_the_anglican_church_of_australia.aspx (accessed March 1, 2016).

Anunobi, Fredoline. "Women and Development in Africa: From Marginalization to Gender Inequality." *African Social Science Review* 2, no. 2 (2002).

Bakke, Dennis. *Joy at Work: A Revolutionary Approach to Fun on the Job*. Seattle, WA: PVG, 2005.

Bakke, Lowell. *A Letter to Rowanna*. Overture: Fresno. [lecture], Bakke Graduate University, Fresno, CA, October 2013.

Bakke, Raymond J. and Jon Sharpe. *Street Signs: A New Direction in Urban Ministry*. Birmingham, AL: New Hope Publishers, 2006.

Banks, Robert J. and R. Paul Stevens, eds. *The Complete Book of Everyday Christianity: An a-to-Z Guide to Following Christ in Every Aspect of Life*. Downers Grove, IL: InterVarsity Press, 2007.

Baur, John. *2000 Years of Christianity in Africa: An African History, 62-1992*. Nairobi, Kenya: Paulines, 2005.

Benvenuti, Sheri R. "Pentecostal Women in Ministry: Where Do We Go from Here?". Cyberjournal for Pentecostal-Charismatic Research http://www.pctii.org/cyberj/cyberj1/ben.html (accessed March 1, 2016).

Block, Peter. *Stewardship: Choosing Service over Self-Interest*. San Francisco: Berrett-Koehler Publishers, 1993.

_____. *Community: The Structure of Belonging*. San Francisco: Berrett-Koehler Publishers, 2008.

Community: The Structure of Belonging. San Franscisco: Berret-Koehler Publishers 2008 Quoted in Evangeline "Smith. An Abode of Abundance. The Positive Outlook of Marginalized Communities (Term Paper, ovi, Bakke Graduate University, 2010).
BringBack Our Girls, 276 School Girls Abducted On April 14, 2014 http://www.bringbackourgirls.ng (Accessed, May 9, 2016)

Charismatic Renewal Ministries. *The Constitution of Charismatic Renewal Ministries*. Owerri, Nigeria: Charismatic Forum Publication, 2004.

Cole, Edwin Louis. *Maximized Manhood*. Port Harcourt, Nigeria: Outreach Christian Bookcentres, 2003.

Covey, Stephen R. *The 7 Habits of Highly Effective People*. London: Simon & Schuster, 1999.

Dejene, Yeshiareg. "Promoting Women's Economic Empowerment in Africa". AFDB http://www.afdb.org/fileadmin/uploads/afdb/Documents/Knowledge/250 40341-FR-DRAFT-DEJENE.9-15-07DOC.PDF (accessed July 1, 2015).

Dobson, James C. *What Wives Wish Their Husbands Knew About Women*. Wheaton, IL: Tyndale House, 1975.

Dobson James "Low Self-Esteem Among Women" Quoted in Joyce Landorf Heatherley The Frangrance of Beauty, Wheaton, 11:Victor Books, 1973.

Dolan, Catherine S. "The Good Wife." *Journal of Developmental Studies* 37, no. 3 (2001): 37-70.

Domestic Violence Prevention Centre. "Domestic Violence Statistics" http://www.domesticviolence.com.au/pages/domestic-violence-statistics.php (accessed September 1, 2014).

Elliott, Barbara J. *Street Saints: Renewing America's Cities*. Philadelphia: Templeton Foundation Press, 2004.

Ettu, Lawrence O. *A Christian Response to the Problems of Single Female Adults in the Church*. Owerri, Nigeria: Charismatic Renewal Ministries, Inc., 2000.

_____. *A Case for Authentic Christian Morality in Africa*. Owerri, Nigeria: Charismatic Forum Publications, 2010.

Eyo, Isidore E. and Hyacinth U. Obi-Keguna, eds. *A Handbook of Psychology: An African Orientation*. Nsukka, Nigeria: Great AP Express Publishers, 2004.

Fatile, Jacob Olufemi, Adejuwon David and Kehinde David. "Gender Issues in Human Resource Management in Nigerian Public Service." *African Journal of Political Science and International Relations* 5, no. 3 (March 2011): 112-119.

Hammond, Sue Annis. *The Thin Book of Appreciative Inquiry*. Plano, TX: Thin Book Pub Co, 1998.

Heatherley, Joyce Landorf. *The Fragrance of Beauty*. Georgetown, TX: Balcony Publishing, 1990.

Hove, Patience Ita. "The Copious Challenges Faced by Women in Leadership in the Zimbabwean Society." Dissertation, Bakke Graduate University, 2012.

Ilechukwu, Adeola Olukemi. "Mentoring as a Tool for Raising Servant Leaders." Dissertation, Bakke Graduate University, 2011.

Ilechukwu, Cosmas. *The Church of His Vision*. Owerri, Nigeria: Cannif Trust Ltd., 2002.

Jenkins, Philip. *The New Faces of Christianity: Believing the Bible in the Global South*. New York: Oxford University Press, 2006.

Jewett, Paul King. *The Ordination of Women: An Essay on the Office of Christian Ministry*. Grand Rapids, MI: Eerdmans, 1980.

Kore, Danfulani Zamani. *Culture and the Christian Home: Evaluating Cultural Marriage and Family in Light of Scriptures* Jos, Nigeria: ACTS University of Jos, 1995.

Kroleweic Stanislaw, Black People: A History of World Polyandry" http://detestee.com/threads/a history-of world-polyandry. 371131 (Accessed May 9, 2016).

Larewaju, Kolade. "Nigeria Has Implemented Five Percent (5%) of Affirmative Action on Women". Feminista News http://www.vanguardngr.com/2015/07/nigeria-has-implemented-only-five-percent-of-affirmative-action-on-women-okunuga/ (accessed August 2015).

Maggay, Melba Padilla. *Transforming Society: Reflections on the Kingdom and Politics*. Quezon City, Philippines: Institute for Studies in Asian Church and Culture, 2004.

Marshall, I. Howard, R.A. Millard, I.J. Parker and D. J. Wiseman. *New Bible Dictionary*. Leicester, England: InterVarsity Press, 1996.

Maxwell, John C. *The 21 Indispensable Qualities of a Leader: Becoming the Person That People Will Want to Follow*. Nashville: T. Nelson, 1999.

Mbajiorgu, Magnus. *The Making of a Disciple*. Lagos, Nigeria: Change Publications, 2005.

McClory, Robert. "Pope Francis and Women's Ordination". National Catholic Reporter, http://ncronline.org/blogs/ncr-today/pope-francis-and-womens-ordination (accessed March 1, 2016).

McPhadden, Patricia. "Development: Marginalization of African Women Deplored". Inter Press Service http://www.ips.org/TV/beijing (accessed June 20, 2015).

Medel-Anonuevo, Carolyn. "Women, Education and Empowerment: Pathways Towards Autonomy". UNESCO Institute of Education, Hamburg, Germany http://unesdoc.unesco.org/images/0010/001006/100662e.pdf (accessed July 1, 2015).

Mensah, Joseph. *The Woman of the Spirit*. Owerri, Nigeria: Charismatic Forum Publications, 2013.

Mensah, Joseph and Francisca Mensah. *Kingdom Principles for Success in Marriage*. Ibadan, Nigeria: Inspiration House Publishing, 2011.

Ngex, "Boko Haram," http://www.ngex.com/nigeria/bokoharam.htm (accessed May 9, 2016)

Obasi, Emmanuel. "Discrimination against Women and Marginalization in Nigerian Politics". Gistarea http://www.gistarea.com/discrimination-women-marginalization-nigeria-politics (accessed August 15, 2014).

Odeydepo, Faith A. *The Effective Minister's Wife*. Canaan Land Ota, Nigeria: Dominion Publishing House, 2008.

Odogwu, Odogwu Emeka. "Nigeria: Anglican Archbishop Okays Women's Ordination to the Diaconate". Virtue on Line: The Voice for Global Orthodox Anglicanism http://www.virtueonline.org/nigeria-anglican-archbishop-okays-womens-ordination-diaconate (accessed March 1, 2016).

Okeke John, "Stakeholders Demand Improved Women Empowerment In post Millenium Development Goals Framework." http: //.guardian.ng//appointments stakeholders-demand-improved women-empowerment-in-post-

Ouellette, Stephanie. "Definition: Women Empowerment". Self Growth http://www.selfgrowth.com/articles/Articles_Women_Empowerment.ht ml (accessed August 1, 2015).

Pakaluk, Michael. "Against Christopher Rollston" http://michaelpakaluk.com/2012/10/14/against-christopher-rollston/ (accessed June 5, 2014).

Rollston, Christopher. "The Marginalization of Women: A Biblical Value We Don't Like to Talk About". Huffpost Religion http://www.huffingtonpost.com/christopher-rollston/the-marginalization-of-women-biblical-value-we-dont-like-to-talk-about_b_1833648.html (accessed June 5, 2014).

Rylko, Stanislaw. "Empowerment of Women in the Church and Society". Council for the Laity, Vatican City, Rome http://www.laici.va/content/dam/laici/documenti/rylko/english/empower ment-of-women.pdf (accessed June 2, 2015).

Sanders, J. Oswald. *Spiritual Leadership: Principles of Excellence for Every Believer*. Chicago: Moody Publishers, 2007.

Scorsone, Suzanne. *The Church Has Defended Women's Rights for 2,000 Years*. UN Commission on the Status of Women. [lecture], March 3, 1998, http://www.cco.caltech.edu/~nmcenter/women-cp/church_empowers_women.html (accessed July 1, 2015).

Sensing, Tim. *Qualitative Research: A Multi-Methods Approach to Projects for Doctor of Ministry Theses*. Eugene, OR: Wipf & Stock Pub, 2011.

Shearlaw Maeve, "Guardian Africa Network. #BringBackOurGirls Campaign Make a Difference in Nigeria? http://www. the guardian.com/world/2015/apr/14/Nigeria-bringbackourgirls-campaign-one-year-on. (accessed May 9, 2016)

Silver, Hilary. "Social Exclusion: Comparative Analysis of Europe and Middle East Youth Initiative". Meyi http://www.meyi.org/uploads/3/2/0/1/32012989/silver_-_social_exclusion-comparative_analysis_of_europe_and_middle_east_youth.pdf (accessed August 1, 2015).

_____. "Social Exclusion and Social Solidarity: Three Paradigms." *International Labour Review* 133, no. 5-6 (1994): 531-578.

Smith, Evangeline. "An Abode of Abundance: The Positive Outlook of Marginalised Communities." Seattle, WA: Bakke Graduate University, 2010.

The Church of England. "The Women Priests Debate" https://www.churchofengland.org/our-views/women-bishops/the-women-priests-debate.aspx (accessed March 1, 2016).

Udegbe, I. Bola. *Gender and Leadership: Image and Reality*. Ibadan: Vantage Publishers, 1998.

Ukachi, Austen C. and Enoch Adejare Adeboye. *The Best Is yet to Come: Pentecostal and Charismatic Revivals in Nigeria. From 1914 to 1990s*. Nigeria: Summit Press, Ltd., 2013.

UNICEF. "Child Trafficking" http://www.unicef.org/nigeria/children_1939.html (accessed April 1, 2014).

United Nations. "Guidelines on Women's Empowerment". United Nations Population Information Network (POPIN) http://www.un.org/popin/unfpa/taskforce/guide/iatfwemp.gdl.html (accessed July 1, 2014).

United Nations Global Impact. "Endorse the Women's Empowerment Principles" https://www.unglobalcompact.org/take-action/action/womens-principles (accessed August 1, 2015).

United Nations Statistics Division. "Violence against Women" http://unstats.un.org/unsd/demographic/products/Worldswomen/WW201 0%20Report_by%20chapter(pdf)/violence%20against%20women.pdf (accessed July 1, 2014).

Veracity. "Nigerian Census - Gender Population Distributon Shift, a Red Flag" http://nigerianpolity.blogspot.com/2007/01/nigerian-census-gender-population.html (accessed September 7, 2014).

Watkins, Jane Magruder, Bernard J. Mohr and Ralph Kelly. *Appreciative Inquiry: Change at the Speed of Imagination.* San Francisco: Pfeiffer, 2011.

Wilde, W. H., Joy W. Hooton and B. G. Andrews. *The Oxford Companion to Australian Literature.* Melbourne: Oxford University Press, 1994.

Wood Braemen, "What is the Islamic State?"http://www.the atlantic.com/magazine/ archieve/2015/03/what-isis-really-wants. 384980 (accessed May 9, 2016).

Women Entrepreneurs Association of Nigeria, ed. *Women Anti-Poverty Project*. Lagos, Nigeria: Ivory Agency Limited, 2009.

World Health Organization. "Violence against Women" http://www.who.int/mediacentre/factsheets/fs239/en/ (accessed July 1, 2015).

World Population Review. "Nigeria Population 2014" http://worldpopulationreview.com/countries/nigeria-population/ (accessed September 6, 2014).

Wright R. Donald. "Slavery in Africa." http: encarta.msn.com 2000 (accessed May 9, 2016).
Ziglar, Zig. *Over the Top*. Nashville: Thomas Nelson, 1997.

www.ingramcontent.com/pod-product-compliance
Lightning Source LLC
Chambersburg PA
CBHW071807090426
42737CB00012B/1990